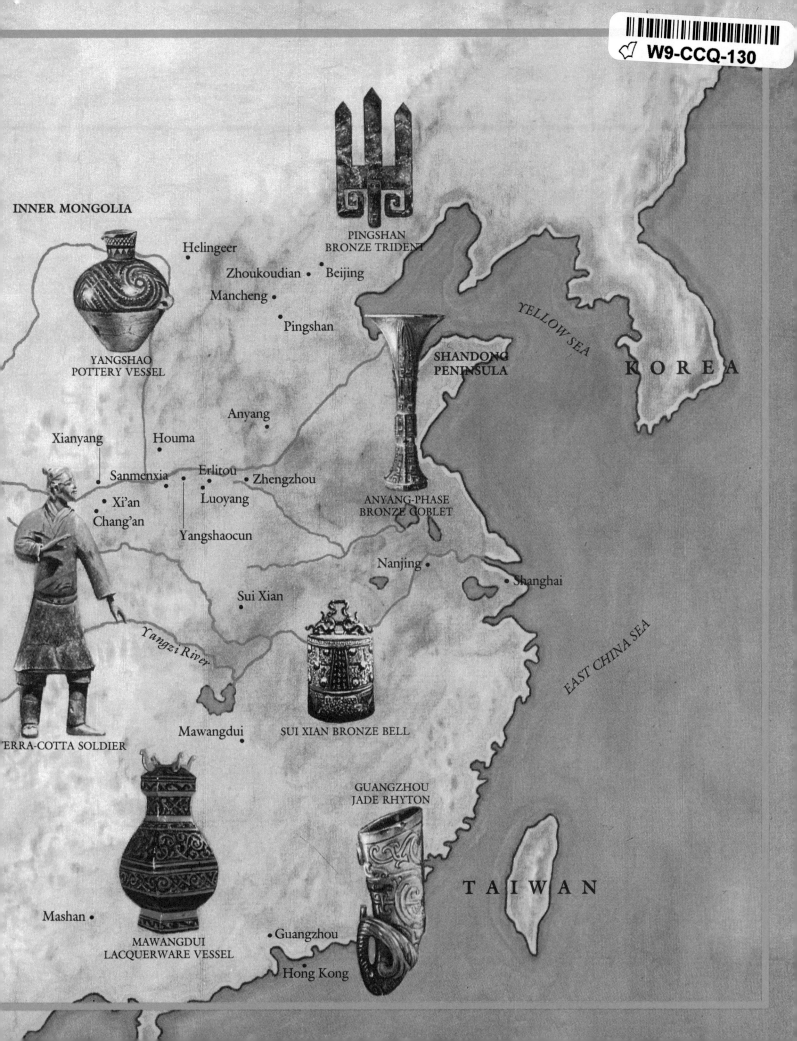

INNER MONGOLIA

PINGSHAN
BRONZE TRIDENT

Helingeer

Zhoukoudian • Beijing

Mancheng •

Pingshan

YANGSHAO
POTTERY VESSEL

YELLOW SEA

SHANDONG
PENINSULA

K O R E A

Anyang

Xianyang   Houma

Sanmenxia   Erlitou
                        Zhengzhou

Xi'an   Luoyang

Chang'an

Yangshaocun

ANYANG-PHASE
BRONZE GOBLET

Nanjing

Shanghai

Sui Xian

EAST CHINA SEA

Yangzi River

TERRA-COTTA SOLDIER

Mawangdui   SUI XIAN BRONZE BELL

GUANGZHOU
JADE RHYTON

T A I W A N

Mashan •

MAWANGDUI
LACQUERWARE VESSEL

• Guangzhou

Hong Kong

Cover: Attired in an intricately arranged military bonnet indicative of his high rank, a bewhiskered commander in the First Emperor's terra-cotta army projects some of the power that enabled the real army to achieve the ruler's goal of uniting China. Behind the officer rises a 51-inch-tall replica of an Eastern Han tower, typical of those used for protective purposes during the tumultuous period.

End paper: Painted on a silklike fabric by the artist Paul Breeden, the map of ancient China displays significant archaeological sites over a 5,000-year-span, from Neolithic times to the Han dynasty, and certain representative artifacts such as a Shang bronze head, a Qin terra-cotta soldier, and a Han jade vessel. Breeden also painted the vignettes illustrating the timeline on pages 158-159.

CHINA'S
BURIED
KINGDOMS

TIME-LIFE BOOKS

EDITOR-IN-CHIEF: Thomas H. Flaherty
Director of Editorial Resources: Norma E. Shaw (acting)
Executive Art Director: Ellen Robling
Director of Photography and Research: John Conrad Weiser
Editorial Board: Dale M. Brown, Janet Cave, Roberta Conlan, Robert Doyle, Laura Foreman, Jim Hicks, Rita Thievon Mullin, Henry Woodhead

PRESIDENT: John D. Hall

Vice President and Director of Marketing: Nancy K. Jones
Editorial Director: Russell B. Adams, Jr.
Director of Production Services: Robert N. Carr
Production Manager: Prudence G. Harris
Director of Technology: Eileen Bradley
Supervisor of Quality Control: James King

Editorial Operations
Production: Celia Beattie
Library: Louise D. Forstall
Computer Composition: Deborah G. Tait (Manager), Monika D. Thayer, Janet Barnes Syring, Lillian Daniels
Interactive Media Specialist: Patti H. Cass

Time-Life Books is a division of Time Life Incorporated

PRESIDENT AND CEO: John M. Fahey, Jr.

Library of Congress Cataloging-in-Publication Data
China's buried kingdoms / by the editors of Time-Life Books.
    p. cm.—(Lost civilizations)
Includes bibliographical references and index.
ISBN 0-8094-9891-X (trade)
ISBN 0-8094-9892-8 (lib. bdg.)
1. China—Antiquities.
2. Excavations (Archaeology)—China.
3. China—Civilization. 4. Tombs—China.
I. Time-Life Books. II. Series.
DS715.C453 1993
931—dc20   93-15068

LOST CIVILIZATIONS

SERIES EDITOR: Dale M. Brown
Administrative Editor: Philip Brandt George

Editorial staff for: *China's Buried Kingdoms*
Art Director: Susan K. White
Picture Editor: Marion Ferguson Briggs
Text Editor: Charlotte Anker
Writers: Denise Dersin, Charles J. Hagner
Associate Editors/Research: Constance Contreras, Patricia A. Mitchell
Assistant Editor/Research: Mary Grace Mayberry
Assistant Art Director: Bill McKenney
Senior Copyeditor: Jarelle S. Stein
Picture Coordinator: David A. Herod
Editorial Assistant: Patricia D. Whiteford

Special Contributors: Beryl Lieff Benderly, Douglas Botting, Charles S. Clark, John Cottrell, Ellen Galford, Lydia Preston Hicks, Janis Johnson, Susan L. Morse, Elizabeth J. Sherman, Terry J. White (text); Tom DiGiovanni, Ann-Louise Gates, Carol Forsyth Mickey (research); Roy Nanovic (index).

Correspondents: Elisabeth Kraemer-Singh (Bonn), Christine Hinze (London), Christina Lieberman (New York), Maria Vincenza Aloisi (Paris), Ann Natanson (Rome). Valuable assistance was also provided by Corky Bastlund (Copenhagen); Bing Wong (Hong Kong); Judy Aspinall (London); John Dunn (Melbourne); Elizabeth Brown, Kathryn White (New York); Ann Wise (Rome); Mary Johnson (Stockholm); Donald Shapiro (Taipei); Dick Berry, Mieko Ikeda (Tokyo). Special thanks to Forrest Anderson in Beijing, whose dedication made this volume possible.

The Consultants:
Dr. Jenny F. So is associate curator of ancient chinese art for the Freer Gallery of Art and the Arthur M. Sackler Gallery of the Smithsonian Institution in Washington, D.C. She has written extensively on the art of ancient China and has mounted exhibitions in both the United States and Canada.

Dr. Robert L. Thorp, associate professor of art history and archaeology at Washington University in St. Louis, has studied the bronze ritual vessels, burials, and architecture of the Shang, Qin, and Han dynasties for 20 years. Since 1991 he has chaired a committee coordinating cooperative research between Chinese and American archaeologists.

Other Publications:

WEIGHT WATCHERS. SMART CHOICE RECIPE COLLECTION
TRUE CRIME
THE AMERICAN INDIANS
THE ART OF WOODWORKING
ECHOES OF GLORY
THE NEW FACE OF WAR
HOW THINGS WORK
WINGS OF WAR
CREATIVE EVERYDAY COOKING
COLLECTOR'S LIBRARY OF THE UNKNOWN
CLASSICS OF WORLD WAR II
TIME-LIFE LIBRARY OF CURIOUS AND UNUSUAL FACTS
AMERICAN COUNTRY
VOYAGE THROUGH THE UNIVERSE
THE THIRD REICH
THE TIME-LIFE GARDENER'S GUIDE
MYSTERIES OF THE UNKNOWN
TIME FRAME
FIX IT YOURSELF
FITNESS, HEALTH & NUTRITION
SUCCESSFUL PARENTING
HEALTHY HOME COOKING
UNDERSTANDING COMPUTERS
LIBRARY OF NATIONS
THE ENCHANTED WORLD
THE KODAK LIBRARY OF CREATIVE PHOTOGRAPHY
GREAT MEALS IN MINUTES
THE CIVIL WAR
PLANET EARTH
COLLECTOR'S LIBRARY OF THE CIVIL WAR
THE EPIC OF FLIGHT
THE GOOD COOK
WORLD WAR II
HOME REPAIR AND IMPROVEMENT
THE OLD WEST

For information on and a full description of any of the Time-Life Books series listed above, please call 1-800-621-7026 or write:
Reader Information
Time-Life Customer Service
P.O. Box C-32068
Richmond, Virginia 23261-2068

This volume is one in a series that explores the worlds of the past, using the finds of archaeologists and other scientists to bring ancient peoples and their cultures vividly to life.

Other volumes included in the series are:

Egypt: Land of the Pharaohs
Aztecs: Reign of Blood & Splendor
Pompeii: The Vanished City
Incas: Lords of Gold and Glory
The Holy Land
Mound Builders & Cliff Dwellers
Wondrous Realms of the Aegean
The Magnificent Maya
Sumer: Cities of Eden

All Chinese words in this volume have been rendered into English following the Pinyin system of transliteration.

CHINA'S BURIED KINGDOMS

By the Editors of Time-Life Books

TIME-LIFE BOOKS, ALEXANDRIA, VIRGINIA

CONTENTS

THE SHANG: A PEOPLE RESCUED FROM OBLIVION

Exquisite example of early lapidary art, this long-tailed jade phoenix was found in the 13th-century BC burial chamber of a Shang king's consort. It was probably worn as an ornament.

The valley of the Huan River is wide and flat, green when the spring crops of the farming collectives sprout in the fertile soil, parched and dusty under the baking sun of a northern China summer. On the river's south bank spreads Anyang. This modest provincial town has a railway station, but it is hardly the place where one would expect travelers from around the world to alight. Yet hundreds of visitors come here each year with one purpose in mind—to see the remains of one of the great civilizations of ancient China, the more than three-millennium-old capital of Shang that lies less than two miles northwest of town.

Almost everything about Shang was once dubious, including the name, which, in ancient texts, applied to a venerated and well-remembered Bronze Age dynasty, to its capital city, and later to the civilization created under its reign. The writings indicated that the line of Shang kings had extended over approximately 650 years, from about 1700 to around 1050 BC, and that their capital had been shifted five times in the early days of the dynasty before its nineteenth king settled at Yin, near Anyang. For almost three millennia, the area around Anyang went by the name of the Ruins of Yin. Today, thanks to those ruins, the area is recognized as one of the world's foremost archaeological sites. It is also one of the most dug.

From the late 1920s onward, for nearly half a century, the

Anyang region experienced almost continuous excavation. When the Anyang Archaeological Team arrived in the spring of 1976 to explore further, some members might have wondered if there was anything of significance left to find. The landscape was pocked with refilled trenches and pits interspersed with scattered heaps of excavated earth. The dig's director, Zheng Zhenxiang, set her team to work on a patch of land slightly elevated above the surrounding fields. There agricultural workers had found a number of Shang remains during the preceding winter. As the season progressed, excitement mount- ed, for the archaeologists began to unearth a series of unsuspected structures. Among these were the foundations of 12 or so houses, 80 storage pits, and more than a dozen tombs. These tombs were built below ground, in the ancient Chinese fashion, with walls and floors of rammed earth created by pounding loose soil solid.

It was the tomb logged Number Five on the site inventory that caused the greatest stir among the excavators. As they worked their way down to the bottom of the pit, about 24 feet below the surface, it soon became clear that this was no ordinary burial. Larger and more elaborate than all the other tombs of that season's dig, Number Five would turn out to be not only a royal grave but also the only properly excavated Shang royal tomb that had not been plun- dered by the robbers who had ravaged the area for 3,000 years.

Among the tomb's multiple and marvelously varied burial goods were some 440 bronze artifacts, 590 jades, 560 bone objects, numerous ivory carvings, a few pieces of pottery, and about 7,000 cowrie shells from the South and East China seas, which had prob- ably been amassed and used as a form of currency. More than twice as many bronzes came out of this one tomb than from all the graves scientifically excavated at Anyang during the preceding decades— mirrors, ceremonial vessels, bells, and weapons, all well crafted and intricate in design. An elaborately decorated bronze cooking stand, with soot still coating its legs, together with three steamer pots, constituted the first such set ever found in China. Among the jades were ceremonial articles and personal ornaments, including exquisite figurines of people and such animated beasts as coiled dragons, crouching bears, and trumpeting elephants.

The archaeologists were not surprised to make a discovery of another sort in the tomb: the remains of 16 humans—men, women, and children—and six dogs, slaughtered for the benefit of the tomb's occupant. Human sacrifice had been common in Shang times.

The splendor of the funerary objects in Tomb Number Five indicated that the individual buried there had been someone of immense distinction within the royal house of Shang. Nothing was left of the corpse, for it had disintegrated during its three-millennium interment. But when inscriptions on tomb objects were deciphered, the identity of the person instantly became clear—hers was a name that had been written on animal bones and tortoise-shells found at other Anyang sites.

The personage thus commemorated was no less than Fu Hao, known to be one of the favorite and most influential of the wives of the Shang king Wu Ding, who ruled throughout much of the 13th century BC. During the 59-year reign ascribed to him, Wu Ding had devoted great energy to dispatching and commanding military expeditions. At least two of these campaigns may have been led by his consort Fu Hao, a general in her own right. As inscriptions found elsewhere revealed, this remarkable woman had commanded an army of 13,000 against the Qiang tribes in the west, a traditional enemy of the Shang, and headed a foray against Tu Fang, a northwestern state. Mistress of a landed estate outside the royal capital, Fu Hao also officiated at some of the rituals at court dedicated to the spirits and to Shang ancestors, a duty that fell only to the most esteemed members of the royal clan. When Fu Hao died, Wu Ding was said to have been heartbroken. Traditional accounts record that he wept copious tears at her funeral and often dreamed of her.

For millennia the mysterious Shang had stirred the imaginations of Chinese antiquarians, a subject of speculation and fantasy. The Chinese philosopher Confucius, as far back as the sixth century BC, said of the Shang: "How can we talk about their ritual? There is a lack of both documents and learned men." Still greater was the skepticism of early 20th-century historians. They dismissed as legend the ancient writings, which placed the Shang in the middle of three

A map of modern China includes its 23 provinces, three municipalities, and five autonomous regions. Although ancient China, the subject of this book, was not divided up thusly, today's boundaries and names are given here in order to help the reader locate the general area of archaeological sites mentioned in the text.

dynastic periods, revered as the "Golden Age" of ancient China. The other two were the Xia, preceding it, and the Zhou, which followed. Disregarding the first two, many historians and archaeologists believed that Chinese history began with the Zhou dynasty.

One reason for this widespread skepticism was the absence of visible monuments. No Xia or Shang temples or palaces survived, which is not surprising, considering how each succeeding dynasty would wind up destroying its predecessor's edifices and building upon the ruins. For the Shang, that destruction included the ransacking of the dynasty's archives when the capital was stormed by the conquering Zhou around 1050 BC and the dispersal of any material that survived. Not until archaeologists began seriously to unearth China's past did the long-blurred outlines of the country's ancient history start to come into focus.

As the tempo of discovery has increased, the detail has sharpened. Today, literally thousands of sites across China are being investigated. Only a few years ago an illustrated book with a sweep as broad as this one—which covers some 5,000 years, ranging from the Neolithic period around 5000 BC to AD 220 and the collapse of the mighty Han—would have been difficult to bring off. But thanks to numerous new finds, the volume can examine the Neolithic and Shang eras, and it can explore in some depth the Western Zhou, an age that saw a refinement of Shang culture; the Eastern Zhou, a time of philosophy, innovation, and constant warfare; the short-lived epoch of Qin, when the First Emperor conquered, consolidated, and centralized much of what is China today; and the glorious Han, a sophisticated, literate age that prospered from the fruits of its own inventiveness as well as its inheritance from past generations.

Archaeologists working in China can consider themselves blessed if for no other reason than that the Chinese of the far distant past went to their graves with burial goods from daily life. Even the poorest might be accompanied by a couple of coins to buy entry to the hereafter or special treatment there. Two motivations spurred the inclusion of such items. Most important was the ancient notion that an individual's ancestors lived on in a spirit world, a realm whose powers could be tapped to advantage only by those among the living who had continued to show their departed forebears proper respect. After the Shang period, people believed that their relatives had to be accorded the means to live comfortably in the afterlife; only thus could a descendant hope to consult them for advice or favors later.

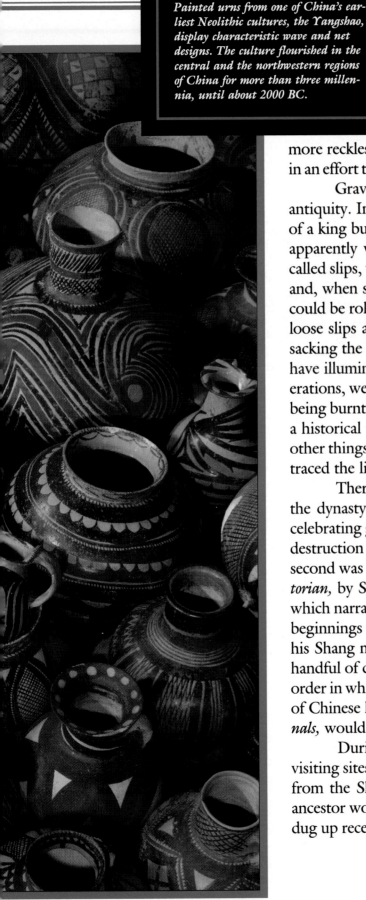

China's enormous underground heritage was long protected, in some cases, by potent taboos relating to the veneration of ancestors, which kept people from disturbing the graves of the dead. Yet always there have been individuals, more reckless than the rest, prepared to risk the wrath of the spirits in an effort to lay their hands on the treasures concealed in the tombs.

Graverobbers could hardly be expected to be respectful of antiquity. In AD 281, for example, when they broke into the tomb of a king buried in the third century BC, they found a collection of apparently worthless slices of bamboo with writing on them, so-called slips, which were traditionally used for recording information and, when strung together with silk ribbons to form lengthy texts, could be rolled into tubes. The robbers gathered up handfuls of the loose slips and set them ablaze as torches to provide light for ransacking the tomb for more valuable loot. Thus treasures that might have illuminated the way back into the past, for untold future generations, were reduced to ash within minutes. The slips that escaped being burnt were retrieved shortly thereafter and found to be part of a historical text that became known as the *Bamboo Annals.* Among other things, they contained a hitherto unsuspected chronology that traced the lineage of the Shang kings.

There were two other documents of consequence concerning the dynasty. One was the *Book of Documents,* a collection of texts celebrating great deeds of the early Zhou kings, which described the destruction of the Shang people by their Zhou conquerors. The second was a monumental first-century BC work, *Records of the Historian,* by Sima Qian, grand historian of the Han emperor's court, which narrated the full sweep of the Chinese past from its legendary beginnings to Sima Qian's own day. He had made what he could of his Shang material—an outline containing a royal genealogy and a handful of documents with references to a few events. He listed the order in which the kings of Shang ruled, and for the next 1,000 years of Chinese history, Sima Qian's text, together with the *Bamboo Annals,* would be the major sources on the Shang.

During the Song dynasty (AD 960-1279), scholars took to visiting sites suggested by ancient texts and collecting bronze vessels from the Shang and Zhou dynasties that had been used in ritual ancestor worship and buried with the dead. Most of these had been dug up recently by farmers and graverobbers and had come into the

11

possession of dealers or connoisseurs. Besides transcribing the inscriptions, the scholars made notes on the locations of the finds—including the sites of former temples and monuments nearby—and described the region's topography. Catalogs were compiled to record all that could be learned about the pieces, and even today these compilations are considered an important resource. A 12th-century Song ruler, Emperor Huizong, was so taken with the relics that he became absorbed in collecting and studying them; according to one estimate by a contemporary of the monarch, the imperial cache grew to some 10,000 pieces. The emperor's interest lay in what he took to be instructions from his ancestors concerning ancient rituals, for the inscriptions on the bronzes were seen as direct messages from the past, indelibly cast in metal and therefore free from the scribal errors that over generations had corrupted the truth.

As the Song period waned, Mongolian hordes began sweeping into China in devastating numbers, and the study of bronzes effectively ended. In the latter half of the 18th century, interest drifted back to an academic perusal of inscriptions and historical texts. A century later, as China's past still slumbered beneath the earth, another powerful momentum to acquire and pore over ancient Chinese artifacts would build—among strangers in faraway lands.

At the end of the 19th century, several Western explorers began to venture along the ancient Silk Road, where two millennia earlier the precious fabric, along with other desirable goods, had begun to travel under imperial auspices from Chang'an, near modern Xi'an, in Shaanxi Province, through the oases of Central Asia to Persia, and on to Rome *(pages 118-119)*. West of China's Gansu Province, the great deserts of Gobi, Lop, and Taklamakan had buried several abandoned settlements in sand. Europe's treasure-hunting antiquarians held high hopes that they would find remains of ancient Chinese culture preserved in these arid desert lands beyond the modern frontier. In this they were not mistaken.

Among the first to blaze a trail through the desolate regions was a Swedish traveler, Sven Hedin, who between 1895 and 1926 crossed the desert wastes into Central Asia. In the heart of the Taklamakan, he found the ancient oasis settlement of Loulan, which had arisen in Neolithic times, then flourished on the Silk Road from the second century BC until the third century AD, when it ceased to exist *(pages 72-81)*. Close behind Hedin came the German explorer Albert von Le Coq. They emerged from their adventures with camel loads of ancient documents and artifacts and swashbuckling reputations.

These colorful figures were followed by a British Orientalist, Aurel Stein, who between 1899 and 1915 excavated the buried oasis cities and frontier forts of the Central Asian deserts in search of manuscripts. Stein persevered in blazing summer heat and winter cold that froze the ink in his pen. At last in 1907, at Dunhuang, deep in the desert, he made what the West would hail as his greatest discovery and the Chinese would decry as a rape of their heritage.

This oasis settlement, which had in medieval times supported a Buddhist community, was still inhabited. In a cliff honeycombed with grottoes, known as the Caves of the Thousand Buddhas, Stein was shown a secret cache of ancient paper and silk scrolls, some dating to the fifth century AD. By deceit and bribery, he persuaded the guardian of this precious hoard to let him take a selection of scrolls—29 full boxes in all—back to New Delhi and then to London's British Museum. Much of what was left was purloined by a French Orientalist, Paul Pelliot, and others who followed him.

In the wake of Aurel Stein's spectacular discovery, eager archaeologists and adventurers descended on China from abroad in the hope of making finds that would prove to be of comparable importance and value. That they succeeded was largely due to opportunities presented by political events overwhelming the country. By the end of the 19th century, key areas of China had been parceled out to Europeans, Russians, and Japanese for commercial exploitation. This

13

DIGGING IN THE MIDST OF DANGER

Archaeologists drawn to China in the 1920s and 1930s by reports of prehistoric sites found their discipline's usual frustrations compounded by civil war. No one recorded the experience more vividly than Carl Whiting Bishop, an American archaeologist with the Freer Gallery of Art in Washington, D.C.

Bishop, who conducted expeditions to northern and central China from 1923 through 1934, managed in spite of all the obstacles to collect data on Neolithic and Han sites. Of particular interest are his copious journal notes and photographs that vividly portray this turbulent period in China's history.

Born in Tokyo in 1881 to missionary parents, Bishop came to the United States at the age of 16 to complete his education, earning a masters in anthropology at Columbia University. From 1914 to 1918, he was assistant curator of Oriental art at the University of Pennsylvania Museum. He made his first archaeological trip to China in 1915. Bishop enlisted in the U.S. Navy in 1918 and served as assistant naval attaché in China until 1920. In 1922 he became an associate curator at the Freer and the next year led the first of two major expeditions to China.

At Wazhaxie in Shaanxi Province, Bishop concentrated on a major Neolithic site—one mile wide and seven miles long—where peasants reported finding numerous potsherds. Digging in the short spaces between the brutal winters and the hot summers, his team unearthed and meticulously documented plain and painted pottery, stone and bone tools, the remains of circular pit dwellings, and human skulls, now thought to date between 2500 and 2000 BC.

Bishop's meticulousness contrasted with the carelessness the archaeologist observed at an unregulated excavation of a Zhou tomb site in Henan Province, where diggers broke or plundered countless bronze vessels and other grave goods and kept no records.

Political turmoil made Bishop's task vastly harder. Work permits, valid one month, became invalid the next as power shifted. Fear of typhus, bands of deserting soldiers, and marauding bandit gangs—"known for committing depredations and atrocities," noted Bishop—made it hard to keep workers. Local superstitions scared away others. Wrote Bishop: "None would remain overnight at the mound, declaring that it was haunted."

Alarmed by the unstable political situation, the Freer finally brought Bishop home in 1934. Until his death in 1942, Bishop devoted himself to the gallery's great Chinese collection.

Seeming worlds apart from the brewing disorder, Carl Whiting Bishop (far right) poses with two local officials at Yungang, Shaanxi Province, in 1925.

Yoked Chinese workers carry earth from an excavation pit in Yuhe Zhen, Henan, in May 1924. From an Eastern Han tomb here, Bishop uncovered bricks and pottery vessels dating to the first and second centuries AD, while soldiers stood guard against bandits.

Mule-drawn carts transport carefully packed finds some 30 miles from Wanchuan to Yunjing in 1931. A number of the finds were then shipped to the Freer Gallery of Art in Washington, D.C., for its study collection.

Objects being readied for a 1931 exhibit of Neolithic artifacts are laid out on the floor of a library in Shaanxi Province. The sign on the wall can be read as "Act with honor and dignity."

circumstance led to the Boxer Rebellion, an uprising of the Chinese against foreigners in 1900, which was crushed by a military expedition of foreign powers. During the subsequent decade, nationalists channeled the Chinese drive for independence into a revolutionary movement that, in 1911, brought the imperial era to an end and instituted a self-governing republic.

Anxious to develop the financially strapped nation, the new government embarked on an ambitious railway building project; its financing and construction were largely in the hands of foreign companies and their technicians. As it happened, one of the lines cut westward from Luoyang in Henan Province to Xi'an in Shaanxi Province, slicing through some of the richest burial grounds of ancient imperial families to reveal deposits of beautiful bronzes, jades, and ceramic figurines. The foreign engineers began to send these pieces back to Europe; soon a fashion for them was created and a market established. Meanwhile local graverobbers, supported by dealers and collectors, converged on every known site to ransack it and peddle their finds in the antique markets of Shanghai and Beijing. The international business in ancient Chinese artifacts became so profitable that mass-produced forgeries began to appear on the market and then in the world's museums, where some probably remain undetected to this day.

Foreign technicians on construction projects developed an interest in Chinese archaeology as well after exposure to the treasures that kept turning up in the field. J. Gunnar Andersson, for example, was a Swedish geologist making a survey of mineral deposits for the Chinese government. A husky man with a forceful personality, Andersson traveled extensively, exploring the geophysical structure of the land. This led him to two outstanding discoveries in 1921: At Zhoukoudian, 26 miles southwest of Beijing, he came upon fossilized bones of animals, which he believed had been killed by hunters. He suggested the site as one that might contain ancient human remains. Eight years later, Chinese paleontologist Pei Wen Chung, following this lead, would discover the 500,000-year-old human fossils that became known as Peking Man *(pages 18-19)*. Andersson's second spectacular find was at Yangshaocun, south of the Yellow River, in Henan Province. There he identified the first Neolithic culture to be unearthed in China. Named for the place where it was first spotted, the Yangshao culture (c. 5000-c. 2000 BC) would become associated with painted pots found there and at hundreds of

NOT ALL THAT MEETS THE EYE

Bronze vessels from Chinese tombs have been avidly collected for their beautiful shapes and exotic decoration, frequently enhanced by a fine green patina built up over the ages. Their very desirability, however, has made them targets for the unscrupulous. Throughout history graverobbers have been stealing the vessels from burial sites.

In order to meet the 20th-century demand, forgers turned out "ancient" bronzes, using false patinas to provide the pieces with a proper antique appearance. Others made extensive repairs on badly damaged or corroded vessels before selling them.

For years, clever dealers capitalized on some collectors' inability to pick out fakes or to distinguish between pristine and repaired pieces. Even museums fell victim to such fraud. Now modern technology often exposes it.

When examined under the microscope, for example, false patinas generally reveal telltale particle structures, or morphology. Chemical and physical tests, radiocarbon and thermoluminescence dating, and radiography all contribute to identifying suspect pieces. But keenness of mind and eye still matter, as demonstrated by a staff member at the Freer Gallery in Washington, D.C., who noticed that a pale-green vessel on display there closely resembled a photograph of one with a polished black surface. A little bit of detective work revealed that it was indeed the same vessel and that it had been artificially patinated before being sold on the world market, presumably to increase its value.

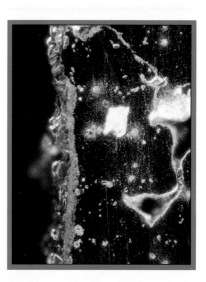

Red and orange particles in this photomicrograph disclose an artificial patina. Natural patinas eat into the bronze and do not just rest on the metal's surface as this one does.

This bronze from Princeton University's Art Museum seemed to be well preserved until a crack exposed recently worked copper covered with traces of sealing wax and solder. The corroded original vessel had been patched extensively, covered by a sand and shellac mixture to simulate encrustation, and stippled with a false patina, still seen in the unstripped half.

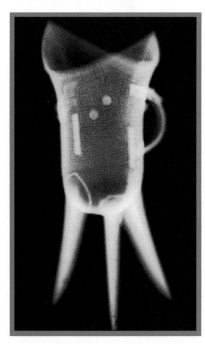

An x-ray radiograph reveals how two legs separated from this wine vessel were reattached with soft-lead solder. Paint matching the original patina camouflaged the repairs.

17

sites along the Wei and Yellow rivers, from the provinces of Gansu to Shandong. Ten years later, Chinese archaeologists would discover a second Neolithic culture, the Longshan (c. 2500–c. 1700 BC), in a village of that name, in Shandong Province. Andersson's finds raised the curtain on a completely unknown aspect of China's past and caused enormous excitement in the scientific community. By demonstrating how effectively fieldwork advanced the investigation of Chinese antiquity, Andersson helped to generate an intellectual climate in which the Chinese themselves would make a great leap forward into archaeological inquiry.

By 1930 a group of Western-trained Chinese archaeologists, with their government's cooperation, were able to put the brake on the fast-developing entrepreneurial activities of foreign expeditions. In that year Aurel Stein, the explorer who had previously made off with numerous artifacts, ran into opposition when his Central Asian expedition attempted to ship out yet another rich collection of antiquities. Restrictions against goods leaving China without proper inspection and approval were now being enforced. After much haggling, Stein was obliged to leave his treasures behind.

Although such laws have been tightened over the years and are, for the most part, effective, China is still struggling to stem the flow abroad of valuable artifacts. Even with a death penalty hanging over their heads, robbers looted 40,000 tombs during a recent two-year period. Museums are also vulnerable to theft, since lack of funds makes proper policing difficult. This is especially true of small county exhibits, where objects discovered in the vicinity are frequently displayed. Thieves may even receive an order for a specific piece, with the "client" sometimes personally awaiting delivery of the purloined object in a boat off the China coast.

While Europeans were hauling away manuscripts and artifacts from the deserts of Central Asia, in the late 19th century a Chinese scholar with a deep respect for his country's past made a discovery that rippled through the academic world and attracted widening circles of attention. The story begins on a day in 1899 when Wang Yirong, of the Imperial Hanlin Academy in Beijing, suffered a bout of malaria. Visiting him at the time was another scholar, Liu Tieyun, who noticed that his friend was dosing himself with a med-

THE CASE OF THE MISSING BONES

In the 1920s and 1930s the world was electrified to learn just how far back in time the roots of China's great civilization stretched. Excavations in caves at Zhoukoudian near Beijing uncovered fossil remains of more than 40 humans (*below*). The bones, nearly half a million years old, were identified as belonging to *Homo erectus,* precursor of *Homo sapiens.* The outbreak of the Sino-Japanese War effectively put a stop to any further digging. As conditions worsened, Chinese officials reportedly asked the U.S. embassy to take the fossils, dubbed Peking Man, abroad for safekeeping.

Boxed, the precious cargo was placed in the care of nine marines headed by train for a steamship. But with the outbreak of World War II, the men were captured, and the bones vanished before they reached the vessel. There are, however, several other versions of the story: One of them claims that the bones were aboard a lighter that sank on its way to the ship; a second that the relics were seized while still on the train and were ground up for medicinal purposes. In the 1950s China accused the United States of hiding the fossils at New York's Museum of Natural History; the "remains" turned out be plaster casts.

Over the years numerous people have come forward claiming to know the whereabouts of the bones. One American woman insisted she had inherited them from her marine husband and agreed to a secret meeting atop New York's Empire State Building. But after demanding a half-million dollars for the remains, she was spooked by the sight of two camera-carrying tourists, became nervous, and eventually fled without offering any solid proof that she indeed had the bones.

icine containing "decayed tortoiseshell" as one of the ingredients. Odder still was the shell that Wang was grinding into his medication, for it bore faint marks that looked like Chinese writing but were so old in form as to be indecipherable. Wang himself had studied bronze inscriptions, and now he saw, to his amazement, that these characters bore a close resemblance to the ones on the vessels.

Their curiosity aroused, Wang and Liu visited the apothecary, who explained that the tortoiseshells came from somewhere in Henan Province. The dealers kept the exact location a secret, but it was believed to be near the town of Anyang. From time to time, apparently, the local farmers turned up ancient shells and bones with plows, selling them as "dragon bones" to apothecaries, who bought them to grind into medicinal powder, hoping it might have, if not magical at least beneficial properties, for the dragon was regarded as an auspicious beast in Chinese folklore. Liu went to all the apothecaries in town and purchased every one of the relics he could find.

Wang collected, through dealers, bones and shells with signs on them. But in 1900 his intense national loyalty brought him to grief and premature death, when he committed suicide at the shaming news of the Western military occupation of Beijing following the Boxer Rebellion. Liu then took over his friend's collection and enlarged on it. In 1903 Liu published lithographs he had made from inscriptions on more than a thousand pieces.

Liu's publication caught the attention of an eminent Chinese scholar by the name of Sun Yirang, who applied his knowledge of ancient bronze inscriptions to unlock the meaning of the signs. The "dragon bones," he declared in a publication in 1917, were in fact oracle bones used by the Shang kings to divine the future, and the inscriptions were records of the topics put to the spirits by the royal diviners and the answers they believed they received in return. His unexpected contact with the utterances of the ancient dynasty of Shang overwhelmed Sun with reverential feelings, and he expressed fascination at how "unexpectedly, in my declining years, I am able to see these marvelous antique traces of ancient inscriptions."

Increased scholarly interest in collecting and studying oracle bones spawned more digs near Anyang by local farmers now employed by curio dealers. Meanwhile scholars continued to work on Liu's pioneer material. One such academ-

A so-called oracle bone bears a Shang message relating to a hunt (above, right). Burn marks on the back of the bone (above, left) reveal where a heated point was applied to predrilled depressions, yielding cracks on the opposite side that a diviner interpreted as a reply.

ic, Luo Zhenyu, supposedly locked himself in his room for 40 days, during which he succeeded in breaking down the contents of the inscriptions into their principal categories, such as names of persons and places. Luo Zhenyu also figured out the method of divining: A topic statement would be written on a bone, usually an ox scapula, or on a tortoiseshell, and a small oval depression would be drilled into the other side. By applying a heated point to the depression, the diviners could cause the bone or shell to crack on the opposite surface. Examining the pattern of fissures, the diviner would "read" the answer to the question posed. Sometimes the diviner inscribed only the topic; at other times the answer would be added; occasionally, a verification citing the outcome would be recorded.

Only the king practiced divining. He might inquire about a dream he had, an illness, the impending birth of a potential heir, or even a toothache. But more often the divinations concerned sacrifice, war, travel, hunting, weather, and harvest—the ruler's communal rather than personal activities. The practice of using oracle bones probably had its origins in the desire to seek the guidance and authority of royal ancestors. Although a court diviner often seems to have interpreted the meaning in the cracks, sometimes the king himself prognosticated. Analysis of diviners' names has revealed that there were at least 120 employed by the Shang kings over the generations.

It was oracle bones from the reign of King Wu Ding that revealed the extent of Fu Hao's activities, including her battle experience. One inscription reads: "The king has mastered his troops and is going to conduct a military campaign with Fu Hao as its commander against Tu Fang this year. Will he be protected?"

The curio dealers were determined to keep their oracle-bone sources a secret. With equal resolve, Luo Zhenyu continued to question them. Through a diligent process of inquiry and deduction, Luo was able to pinpoint the exact place where the bones were being unearthed—the village of Xiaotun, near Anyang, in the area so long called the Ruins of Yin.

Luo's brilliant young assistant, Wang Guowei, added the crucial piece to the puzzle. Wang was able to reconstruct a succession of Shang kings from the evidence of oracle-bone inscriptions. In his scholarly publication of 1917, he showed his list to be almost identical with the king lists preserved for about 2,000 years in Sima Qian's history—final proof that this acclaimed historian had indeed set down accurate records of a genuine Chinese culture predating the Zhou. "Chinese archaeology is shaken to its foundations by this startling revelation," a leading Chinese scholar, Liang Qichao, told a learned meeting in Beijing in October 1926. The new studies of oracle bones, he said, were putting into perspective "many great historical events which are recorded in old books and which have been unintelligible to us and regarded as fantastic and far-fetched."

China's first scientific institute, the Academia Sinica, was established two years later, setting as one of its early tasks a thoroughgoing investigation of the oracle bones. A researcher named Dong Zuobin was sent to Anyang by the institute, with instructions to determine the bones' precise source. He reported that all the farms along the banks of the Huan River had yielded oracle bones and every household in the village had some.

Two days after Dong arrived in Anyang, he hired "a small child" to show him what adults were reluctant to reveal, and "the child pointed to a sand heap and stated that oracle bones came from underneath it," he wrote in his notes. The eastern slope of the large mound, north of Xiaotun village, rose from the riverbank, its top overgrown with yellow grass. Dong's investigation of the area verified the child's report: "After carefully examining the western side of the sand heap, in an area near the cotton field," he wrote, "I found ten newly dug and refilled pits."

Dong spent that autumn digging into the mound, aided by local farm laborers and six colleagues. When he and his party withdrew for the season, they took with them 784 inscribed bones and a growing conviction that there was something far more important to be found there. Both the *Bamboo Annals* and Sima Qian's history suggested this area as the Shang capital. And even had there been no ancient writings, it made sense to assume, as Dong did, that this great concentration of oracle bones would be located near the center of Shang power. His report propelled archaeologists on to the next step, for he concluded it with the statement that "scientific excavation by national scholarly institutions must be undertaken without delay."

Dong Zuobin then turned his attention to the recovery and analysis of oracle bones, in which he was to become a leading expert. Over the ensuing years he personally would collect 28,574 of the 100,000 or so bones that were to emerge from the Anyang area.

Soon after Dong Zuobin's dig, in December 1928, the Academia Sinica's Institute of History and Philology set up an archaeology section under Li Ji, a 33-year-old, Harvard-trained Chinese anthropologist, who took over supervision of the digging at Anyang. In the spring and fall of 1929, Li made two expeditions to Anyang with the financial backing of the Freer Gallery of Art of the Smithsonian Institution in Washington, D.C., tackling his task with archaeological methods that now had worldwide acceptance. Before commencing his first major excavation, Li surveyed the topography of the site with his team of 16, which included several individuals who were to become China's leading archaeologists. By the summer of 1930 the dig was well underway.

Digging at Anyang, however, was fraught with problems. The winters were so cold and the summers so hot that the excavations had to be done in spring and autumn, the windy seasons. Of the effects of the seasonal gales, Herrlee Glessner Creel, an American visiting the Anyang group, wrote, "The yellow dust flies so thick that one can hardly see 10 feet ahead. Goggles must be worn. To wear goggles, in a tearing gale which threatens to fling one to the bottom of 30-foot pits, and under these conditions to supervise the activities of a number of workmen and keep the minute records demanded by scientific archaeology is not easy."

Bandits, drawn from the poverty-stricken peasantry of the surrounding area, were an additional hazard. Some of them had become rich, not so much from the proceeds of looted oracle bones as from the fine Shang bronzes they had pilfered from tombs. One of these bronzes, reported Creel, was being sold by a Beijing antique dealer for $50,000, a big sum in 1935. Creel observed that for the farmer "wealth has brought danger, not happiness." The suddenly wealthy peasants who made such discoveries, he wrote, "hardly dare venture out of doors in the light of noon, for fear of being kidnapped and held for huge ransom."

Police and soldiers patrolling the site only stirred up the resentment of the local people, who felt they were being deprived, by the archaeologists, of what was rightfully theirs. Creel warned of a secret society that rumor held had been

A photograph taken in the 1930s shows excavation of a Shang royal tomb (above). The Chinese archaeologists who worked on the site found remains of sacrificial victims buried along the ramps and, at the bottom of the pit, artifacts of bone, stone, shell, antler, tooth, bronze, and clay where the royal coffin had been.

formed to assassinate the director of excavations. As if this was not enough, the archaeologists were faced with the passionate opposition of respectful Chinese to any digging that might disturb the graves of the dead, no matter how ancient they might be. A high official of the Chinese government, Creel complained, had circulated a message, by telegraph, "protesting in the strongest language against the scientific excavation of ancient tombs."

Despite the obstacles, the team soldiered on into 1931, a season that saw a significant breakthrough, as the archaeologists began to expose the foundations of three major building complexes. The most northerly was later interpreted as the compound of the royal clan. It was located by the bank of the river that flowed through the area and consisted of 15 substantial dwellings of rectangular or square shape. Their foundations were rammed-earth platforms, up to 10 feet thick. Rows of boulders, which had been set on the pounded soil, suggested that wooden pillars, supporting the roof beams, were once raised on these stones. Astonishing was the size of some of the buildings. One structure gave evidence of having extended 280 feet in length and nearly 50 feet in width and must have loomed over the flat landscape of Anyang with imposing majesty. Scattered nearby were the remains of humbler structures—small round or square earthen pits—that may have housed laborers and servants.

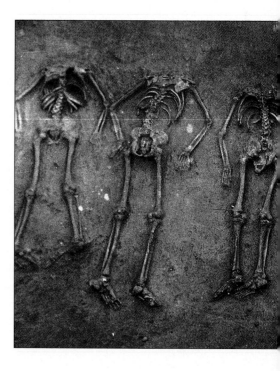

After a few seasons of digging the archaeologists encountered a sight that stunned and dismayed them, as the earth yielded a multitude of skeletons, evidence of human sacrifice. According to Li Ji's writings, it was the first time that scientists had "incontestable confirmation" of "this barbarous custom."

The most momentous excavation began in the fall of 1934, across the river, northwest of the main Anyang site, this time under the direction of Liang Siyong, a member of Li Ji's field staff. Learning that graverobbers had recently made off with rich pickings at that site, Liang decided to switch the season's main effort there—"a momentous decision," Li Ji would write of the shift. Four huge tombs were unearthed in the 1934 season; during the subsequent three years, another six were found, together with more than a thousand lesser burials. All 10 large tombs were identified as royal.

Varying in size, the tombs were deep and rectangular, with access ramps built into the northern and southern sides. Some, however, were laid out in a cruciform plan, with four ramps. While all the tombs had been plundered of most valuables, the tombs themselves

were intact, enabling archaeologists to work out burial details.

When each of the great kings who had been buried here died, a great pit was dug; the largest measured almost 58 feet long, 52 feet wide at the mouth, and 39 feet deep. Earth from such pits was brought out along the ramps that had been cut in the sides. At the bottom of the shaft, a smaller pit was carved out of the soil. Around the sides a ledge of pounded earth was made, and a wooden chamber, some eight feet high, built on it. The coffin containing the dead king was installed inside, surrounded by royal grave goods. The chamber was then closed with a roof of elaborately carved and painted timbers and earth laid on top. Erecting the massive structure must have required a huge, probably conscripted, labor force.

As they dug their way down to the bottom of each royal tomb, the archaeologists came upon sacrifices, human and animal. From these they could reconstruct what had happened after the king was laid to rest. For example, in an 11th and final royal tomb, excavated at nearby Wuguan village in 1950, 41 sacrificial victims were placed in coffins and buried on the ramps leading to the king's tomb—24 women on the west side, 17 men on the east. Then eight dogs were killed—four to guard the lower ends of each of the ramps. Buried in three pits, higher up on each ramp, were eight two-horse teams of chariot horses, with two armed charioteers between each pair. As layers of earth were pounded into the tomb, more sacrificed animals—mostly monkeys and deer—and humans were added. The additional human remains consisted of 34 skulls, all male, placed facing the center of the tomb. South of the royal burial place were 17 mass graves containing 160 decapitated skeletons, whose heads could not be found; among the victims may have been those whose skulls lay inside the tomb. This was by no means an isolated phenomenon; in

The leering face that adorns the Shang bronze ax at top matched the instrument's awful function. Recovered on the entrance ramp of a tomb in Shantung, the ax was one of two used to decapitate 48 sacrificial victims. A similar rite occurred in an Anyang tomb, where the six headless skeletons above turned up.

other tombs, groups of skulls and mutilated skeletons would be uncovered as digging in the area progressed.

For decades scholars have considered the rationale for the taking of life on such a scale—well beyond the number of servants and companions that might reasonably be expected to accompany a king to the afterlife. Oracle bones reveal that human and animal sacrifice was required on occasions other than royal burials. Many of the Anyang inscriptions refer to sacrifices of enemy prisoners of war. People and creatures of all kinds—even elephants and rhinoceroses—were offered to ancestral, as well as mountain and river, spirits. On one occasion more than 1,000 people were put to death in such rites.

To understand human sacrifice in China, it is necessary to understand how the ancient Chinese viewed a king and his ancestral spirits. The ancients, today's scholars argue, believed that royal spirits acted as intermediaries between Shang society and the supreme deity, called Di, or Shang Di. The power of these ancestors—and thus their ability to act on behalf of the kingdom, particularly in guaranteeing military victories—was derived from offerings. Offerings frequently included innocuous items such as wine—which accounts for the large number of ritual vessels recovered from graves *(pages 30-31)*. But the spirits also were nourished with sacrifices of flesh and blood. Hence for the community's sake, a deceased king, promoted by death to ancestor status, had to take sacrificed human beings with him.

There was a prize yet awaiting the Anyang archaeologists equal to anything they had yet uncovered. As fate would have it, the discovery was made on the last day of the 1936 season. In a pit at Xiaotun, bearing the site reference number H127, at 4:00 p.m., on June 12, according to the team's logbook, "numerous tortoiseshells suddenly appeared in H127. When we ended the day at 5:30 p.m., the digging party had cleared in one hour and a half only half a cubic meter of closely packed tortoiseshells." The work was extended for another day, assuming that would give the excavators enough time to finish digging and clearing out the contents of "this amazing archive," as the logbook called it.

It soon became clear, however, that to remove the shells piece by piece would take too long, for they had been stacked in an orderly fashion and after three millennia in the ground they were stuck together in a solid mass. They would have to be dug out as a whole. Working uninterruptedly for four days and four nights, the field team finally detached the more than three-ton block of shells from the soil.

AN INGENIOUS CASTING METHOD

To produce objects of bronze—especially ones as ambitious as the Shang's—required great technological skill. The process used enabled metalsmiths to turn out everything from small ceremonial vessels to bronzes weighing nearly a ton. Called piece-mold casting, it ensured precise detailing, yet allowed walls thin enough to conserve precious metal.

Molds could consist of many pieces, but the simple set shown here serves to demonstrate the method. Work began with a vase-shaped model, complete with decoration. A clay impression, forming the outer mold, was taken of the model and cut

It took more months of patient labor before the shells could be separated and inspected. In the final reckoning 17,096 inscribed pieces had been stored in Pit H127, all but eight of them tortoiseshell. It seemed that most of the archive had been buried in the reign of Wu Ding and was so well preserved that a number of shells still retained the vermilion pigment with which the original inscriptions had been written prior to their being incised in the shell. Besides the sheer volume of information contained on the shells, for Li Ji the unearthing of the archive was "one of the climaxes which seems to have given us a kind of spiritual satisfaction beyond all others."

The joys of such discovery were soon to be suspended, for in 1937 the Japanese invaded North China, and all Chinese work at Anyang stopped. In the years of danger that ensued, many Academia Sinica archaeologists sought safety in remote areas of western China, taking with them notes and photographs. There, in spite of prolonged hardship and ill health, they studied and wrote about the many finds they had made during their years of digging at Anyang.

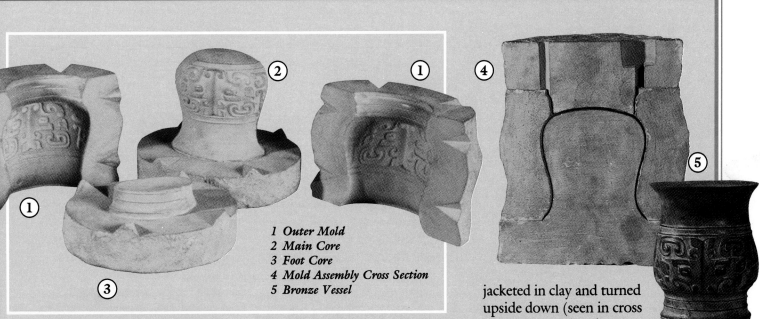

1 Outer Mold
2 Main Core
3 Foot Core
4 Mold Assembly Cross Section
5 Bronze Vessel

into two parts. After triangular keys were created along the edges to ensure a proper fit later, the two segments were fired and assembled so clay could be inserted into the hollow to form a main core. The core was then shaved so there would be space between it and the mold. A separate piece, the foot core, with a pouring gate and a vent for displaced air, was made. Now the mold was reassembled and spacers were added between core and mold to ensure uniform thickness of the yet-uncast vessel. The unit was jacketed in clay and turned upside down (seen in cross section) so molten bronze could be poured in. Less than an hour later, the metal had cooled and the mold could be broken away and the vessel exposed. The removal of the core and a final working of the surface with abrasives left the bronze finished.

STARTLING DISCOVERIES OF A WIDER SHANG WORLD

China's soil seems everywhere sown with the past, and accidental discoveries, often of major significance, keep on occurring. So it happened in July 1986, when brickworkers digging in Sichuan Province, more than 600 miles from the Shang capital at Anyang, brought up some ancient jades with their shovels and hit upon one of the most surprising finds of the decade. Archaeologists called to the site, known as Sanxingdui, began explorations and unearthed a rectangular pit holding some 300 gold, bronze, jade, and stone objects dating to the 13th or 12th century BC—contemporaneous with the Shang culture at Anyang. But many of the relics, including some life-size bronze heads with strikingly angular features, were of a kind never seen before. The presence, in addition, of 13 elephant tusks and a mass of broken and burnt animal bones led the investigators to conclude that the pit was connected with some sort of sacrificial ceremony.

In a second, nearby pit, creat-

Unlike any Shang sculpture ever discovered, the almost nine-foot-tall statue from the Sanxingdui sacrificial pits expresses, in his posture, dress, and elevation on a pedestal, power.

ed a generation or so after the first, the archaeologists turned up a profusion of still stranger objects: a branched bronze "spirit tree" and ornaments apparently designed to hang on it; 41 bronze heads of varying sizes; more than 60 charred elephant tusks; and most unexpectedly, an 8½-foot-tall figure standing on a high base *(left)*. This pit, like the other, was located outside an earthen city wall, built a century or more earlier, that surrounded remains of various structures.

While researchers are still seeking clues to the reason for the pit sacrifices and their intended recipient, the finds made one thing clear: Scholars had vastly underestimated the size and complexity of the Shang-period world. Sanxingdui, while remote from Anyang and culturally distinct, was clearly a major city in its own right, one in contact with far-off neighbors to the north and the east, as evidenced by similarities in motifs on the ceremonial bronze vessels of each. The prevalent notion of Anyang as a lone center of civilization surrounded by barbarians would have to be revised. Indeed, some think other major centers of culture contemporary with the Shang period yet lie buried, awaiting discovery.

The three bronze heads above range from 5 to 18 inches and display exaggerated, angular features and variations in headgear. Some scholars suggest the heads were cast and buried as ritual substitutes for decapitations.

Excavation of Sanxingdui's second sacrificial pit (above, left) reveals tusks strewn among bronze figures and broken pieces of a so-called spirit tree. In another shot (above, right), archaeologists painstakingly uncover an enormous bronze mask. The hand protruding below the head is that of the full-size bronze figure seen on the opposite page. Bulging eyes and bizarre, stylized features mark the bronze face at right, which measures about two feet in height and more than four feet in width.

The end of the war did not bring the longed-for stability. As the Communists tightened their grip on postwar China, some of the veterans of the prewar Anyang digs again sought refuge. Dong Zuobin and Li Ji went to Taiwan, where Li Ji founded the archaeological department of Taiwan University and continued to work on the Anyang finds, publishing the results. The excitement of excavation on the Chinese mainland thus passed to a new generation of Chinese archaeologists, who despite the shifts in ideology and government remained loyal heirs to the scientific tradition founded by Li Ji and his colleagues more than 20 years before.

With the founding of the Chinese People's Republic in 1949, archaeology made a quantum leap into a brilliant and prolific era. On May 24, 1950, new legislation gave protection to cultural relics and monuments, forbade the export of historic works of art, and regulated all archaeological activities throughout the country. Under the Communists, archaeology was deemed a state enterprise, and its study, once virtually unknown in China, became a recognized course

Vestige of a rich ceremonial past, the set of 12 ritual wine vessels below dates from the time of the Zhou conquest of the Shang in the late 11th century BC. Reportedly found in a tomb in 1901, the set was owned until 1911 by the viceroy Duan Fang, seen on the left in the photo at right, before passing to New York's Metropolitan Museum of Art. Having left outlines of their corroded bases on the altar table on which they long stood, some of the vessels could be placed in their original positions for the picture below.

in some Chinese universities. Chinese archaeology would now turn the spotlight on the remains of the poor and lowly of the ancient world, not just the rich and powerful, and a huge increase in finds would follow the massive upsurge in large-scale agricultural projects and industrial construction work throughout the country, which uncovered many new tombs and graves.

In 1950 excavation was resumed at Anyang and continues to the present day. Along with examining spectacular finds such as the tomb of Fu Hao, made in 1976, the new generation of archaeologists has worked meticulously on sifting every scrap of evidence uncovered while probing more than nine square miles of the Anyang region. The mass of archaeological material recovered from the site forms the basis of much of today's knowledge about the Shang.

The Shang were an agricultural people, cultivating millet as their principal grain, using farm implements fashioned from wood and bone. But they developed several technologies and important skills as well that had far-reaching implications for the future. The smelting of bronze—using charcoal as fuel and clay molds to fashion ritual objects and weapons—grew into a major industrial activity *(pages 26-27)*. The Shang worked jade, producing beautiful items from the hard mineral, and from the evidence of traces of silk fabrics preserved on Shang bronzes, it would seem that the Shang had learned how to breed silkworms and spin the fibers. Surveyors of the heavens, the Shang kept a calendar, with the months based on the phases of the moon and the years on the position of the sun. Most important was their written language, inscribed on oracle bones and bronzes as logographs, symbols that represent entire words, which formed the foundation of Chinese writing.

Shang kings often found it necessary to go to war to subdue the states threatening their frontiers. Oracle bones offer clues to military strategies and weapons. They suggest that infantry and archers were organized together in formations consisting of companies of the left, right, and center, each with 100 men. Sacrificial burials of chariots and charioteers indicate that there were companies of five squadrons, each of which had five chariots. Weapons were found with the chariots, in sets. Each set apparently included a bow made of cattle sinews and horns, the height of a man, which probably came

31

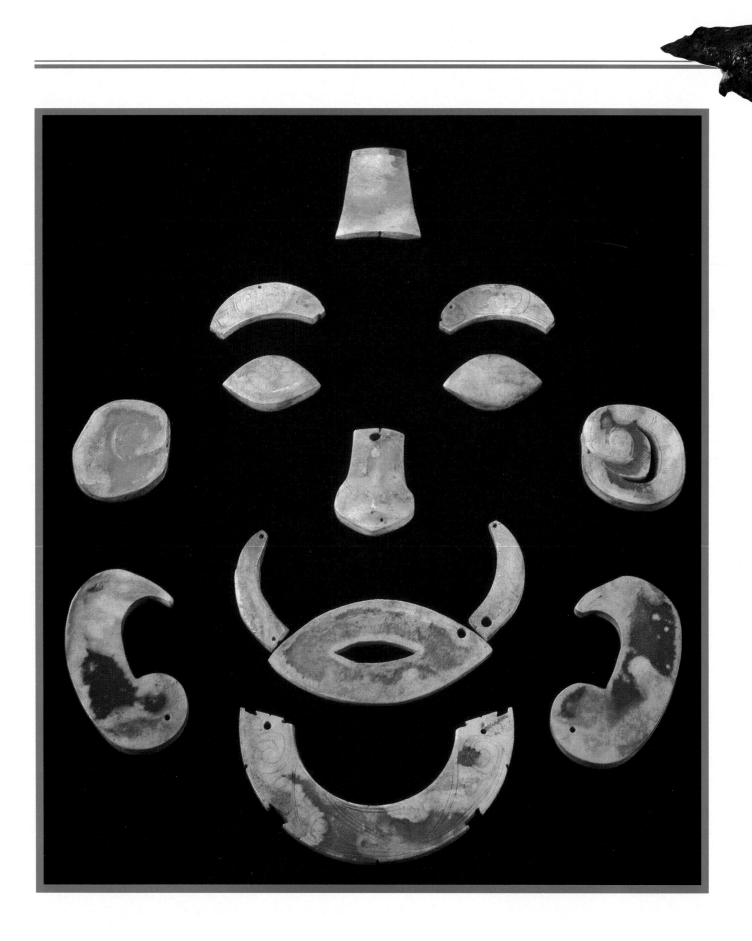

with feathered, wood-shaft arrows half the size of the bow, tipped with sharpened stone, bone, antler, shell, or bronze. In addition there were a small bronze knife, a sharpening stone, a yard-long wood-shafted bronze halberd, and a shield of wood-framed leather, decorated with a tiger pattern.

Archaeologists pondered how, around 1300 BC, this Bronze Age culture could have flowered almost overnight. A partial answer came when, starting in the 1950s, two major pre-Anyang sites were discovered to suggest that Shang roots ran deep. One was a walled city near Zhengzhou in Henan Province. After intensive excavations, some scholars concluded that this was Ao, an early Shang capital; it may have been from here that the kings moved to Anyang. Seventy miles farther west, near modern Yanshi, several sites revealed a still older culture, known as Erlitou. The discovery of what may be a palace at Erlitou, in 1976, has led some scholars to identify this spot with Bo, the first of five Shang capitals, known from ancient writings. Since many cultural elements at these sites are similar to those found at Anyang, scholars have concluded that Erlitou, Zhengzhou, and Anyang represent, respectively, early, middle, and late stages of Shang civilization.

Radiocarbon dates have placed the earliest strata of the Erlitou culture at the end of the third and beginning of the second millennia BC, the period that traditional chronologies assign to the Xia dynasty. The founding of the Shang dynasty is usually dated several hundred years later, around 1700 BC. There has been some debate as to whether the older period at Erlitou represents the Xia, the most historic of the three Bronze Age dynasties described by ancient Chinese writers. The Xia dynasty, said by them to have existed from the 22nd to the 18th centuries BC, remains as veiled from modern view as the Shang was a century ago. Speculations about whether the Xia actually existed can only be settled when inscriptions from this dynastic period—providing the Xia had a written language—begin to accumulate.

If a Xia dynasty did exist, it probably overlapped the Shang period, just as the Zhou—a powerful neighbor to the west that culturally resembled the Shang in many ways—undoubtedly was around during at least the latter part of the Shang period. In the mid-11th century BC, the Zhou had grown strong enough to overrun Shang territory, sack the capital at Anyang, and establish a new dynasty. The conquerors then founded a capital for themselves near Xi'an in Shaanxi Province. Because this capital lay in the west, the earliest phase of Zhou rule has come to be called the Western Zhou period to distinguish it from a later era, the Eastern Zhou, when the Zhou capital was moved to Luoyang in the east. Western Zhou kings were now masters of a vast expanse of China—from Inner Mongolia in the north to the Yangzi River in the south, from Gansu in the west to the Eastern Sea.

Skills and technologies developed by the Shang were advanced by the Western Zhou. In agriculture, the soybean was introduced, and harvests were improved by rotation, which allowed some fields to lie fallow and recover their fertility. Possessing a delight in ritual equal to their predecessors, Zhou rulers continued to have bronze foundries to turn out ceremonial vessels. Many bronze and some oracle-bone inscriptions survive from the Western Zhou period. The bronze writings are often long ones, rich in historical content, for it became the custom for kings to have inscribed on vessels orders given to their officials, as well as their military deeds. Knowledge of bronze making apparently led to the smelting of iron ore and the production of iron items, examples of which have been found recently at Sanmenxia, in Henan Province *(page 33)*.

Above all, Western Zhou rulers consolidated and refined a complex administrative structure that assembled and disbursed military and economic resources, a system to which all future regimes would be indebted. The new kings justified their conquests with an ideology that has underpinned the Chinese state for millennia and may account for its upheavals as well as its conscientious rulers. This was the notion that those in charge held a sacred trust from the supreme deity, which allowed them to rule only in so far as they remained virtuous; if they failed their people, this "mandate of heaven" would be removed by rebellion or outside military intervention.

Under the Shang kings, metallurgy, agriculture, weaponry, art, writing, and other elements of Chinese culture had all flourished. By the time the Western Zhou moved their capital eastward to Luoyang in 771 BC, a firm base had been built for the next brilliant phase of Chinese civilization to occur.

HOMAGE TO ANCESTORS

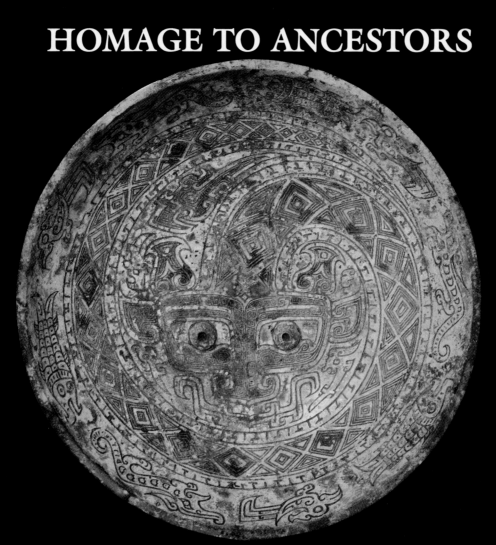

Among some of ancient China's greatest treasures are its bronze ritual vessels. Recovered from graves and tombs, they were used by families 3,000 years ago in ceremonies that honored ancestors. During the approximately 650-year-long Shang period, when the art of making the vessels reached its peak, only the powerful and well-to-do could afford these exquisitely crafted pieces.

Although Shang metalsmiths traditionally concentrated on basic shapes that stemmed for the most part from simple clay Neolithic prototypes, artisans of the Late Shang period learned to enhance the aesthetic value of their work by gracing their output with intricate motifs. A piece such as the fanciful *pan* basin pictured above demonstrates their skill. When the participants in a ceremony dipped into the basin to ritually cleanse themselves, they would have gazed through the water into the large, slightly bulging eyes of the coiled dragon lying on the bottom.

Scholars debate whether the creatures on such elaborate bronzes served anything more than a purely decorative function. According to one theory, the animals depicted were those thought to be capable of assisting shamans' efforts to communicate with the dead.

Under the conquering Zhou, the bronzes began to change in character. Metalsmiths took to producing vessels with inscriptions to commemorate success on the battlefield or hunting ground rather than solely to invoke the names of ancestors. By the end of the Western Zhou period, an entirely different repertoire of decorative elements had emerged, ensuring that the finest vessels of the Late Shang would preserve their uniqueness—and thus achieve their own special immortality.

RITUALS OF BEAUTY AND MYSTERY

"Every custom and rite is observed, every smile, every word is in place." This Zhou poet's comment about ancestor rituals also pertains to the Shang period. Bronze food and wine vessels played an important role in the ceremonies of both dynasties. Old texts describe how members of the family knelt on mats before carefully arrayed vessels that varied in number according to each person's age or rank. Specific pieces were designated for grain offerings and other kinds of food.

The aura of the ceremonies probably depended as much on the quality of the vessels as on the food. The *taotie* mask, seen here in the background, is the principal motif on many bronzes. Always featuring a pair of large eyes, it projects the look of some fantastic beast.

The mysterious, broad human face that appears on each of the four sides of a vessel known as a ding distinguishes it from more numerous vessels with tao-tie masks and animal designs. This one was likely used for cooking meat.

Animal heads at the top of the handles on this gui hold birds in their mouths. Each bird's body rounds out a handle, and its feet and tail appear below on a rectangular extension. An unusually detailed inscription inside the bowl refers to a sacrifice performed for a consort of the fourth to last Anyang king.

With clawed feet and spines jutting menacingly, three precast dragons support the bowl of this ding with their gaping mouths. Tigers decorate each handle, and taotie masks—one of which can be seen here—encircle the bowl.

SPIRITS FOR THE SPIRITS

There is ample evidence to indicate the Shang drank alcohol, cooked with it, and used it in ceremonies. In fact, they employed more varieties of ritual vessels for wine—made from millet and other grains—than for food. In general, their wine vessels seem more elaborate than others used in Shang ceremonies. The rubbing of a turtle seen in the background comes from such a vessel; at its center is a whorl circle that may symbolize fire.

The Shang liked wine warm and heated it in vessels with legs long enough to stand in coals. The Zhou claimed the Shang's over-indulgence in wine made them unfit to rule. Many of the vessel types discontinued by the more abstemious Zhou after they conquered the Shang were those the vanquished used for wine.

This fang jia, *with a cover handle consisting of two birds, displays a taotie mask, an owl, dragons, and whorl circles. The capped posts attached to the sides may have been used to lift the vessel from coals.*

Once a wine vessel, this you contained more than 320 jades when unearthed in 1970; two you found years earlier also had jades inside. The piece is admired for its crisp, sharp casting and the graceful repetition of motifs on its surface.

This he was used for serving and, perhaps, heating wine. A short link attaches the handle to the lid. Stylized dragons and taotie masks cover the surface.

Typically found together, *gu* goblets and *jue* wine pourers such as these crop up in greater numbers in Shang graves than any other ritual vessels. The *gu* shown here typifies the widemouthed design used for more than 500 years. Decoration for the upper portion of the goblet is confined to long, inverted blades. The *jue* rests on the tips of three triangular legs. A pointed extension provides a counterweight for the pouring lip.

40

Held in the grasp of an animal, a man with claws forms part of the decoration on this *you* wine vessel. He may represent a shaman who requires the beast's assistance to cross from the world of the living into that of the dead. Human images on Shang bronzes are extremely rare, which adds to the value of this priceless piece.

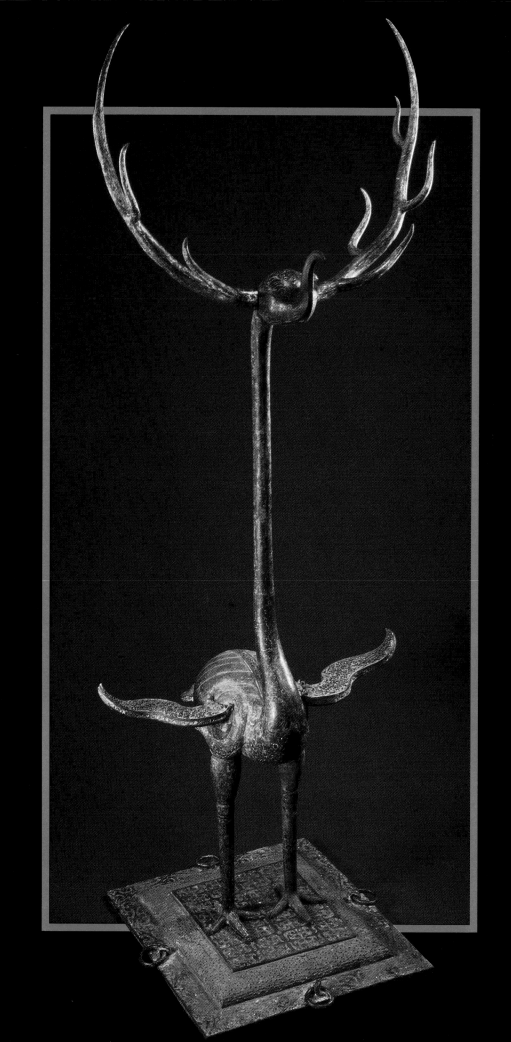

THE EASTERN ZHOU: AN AGE OF CONTRADICTIONS

Occasionally an excavation yields an object that puts the archaeologists uniquely in touch with peoples of the past. So it was with a silver trumpet found in the tomb of the Egyptian pharaoh Tutankhamen and with a little clay ocarina unearthed from a Mayan grave; blown again, the instruments came back to life, their clear tones leaping across the millennia. And such was the case with a set of 26 chiming bells discovered in 1979 in a 2,400-year-old tomb of a Chinese nobleman in the province of Henan. Decorated with dragon motifs, the bells—each capable of sounding two different notes—bore individual inscriptions praising their musical quality. When struck on the lips with mallets or between the centers and the edges, they rang with the liquid sounds that had delighted the noble's ear.

As it so happened, a traveling exhibition of Chinese artifacts was being planned for Seattle, Washington, to open in July 1988, with the chime planned as one of the outstanding displays. Someone had the bright idea that the instrument should be played at the show, but as the curators well knew, continued striking of the bells would surely damage them. A solution was found. The bells were played one at a time in China, and the sounds of each carefully recorded. No one could even guess what the music of the nobleman's court had been like, but the exhibition's organizers commissioned the American

"For Zeng Hou Yi's eternal use" reads an inscription on the beak of this inlaid bronze, antlered crane. Buried with the marquis Yi, the over four-foot-tall fantastic creature may have been intended as a guardian against evil spirits.

composer Norman Durkee to write a piece for the chime, limiting himself to the instrument's notes. This he did, and his composition was played on an electronic keyboard instrument called a sampler, using the bells' replicated tones. On tape the work was used to greet visitors at the exhibition and put them in the proper frame of mind for the treasures they were about to see. What the listeners heard was a mellifluous, modern melody, ringing forth in the tones of a magnificent instrument given renewed vitality by the electronic wizardry of the 20th century.

Similar chimes were owned by many other Chinese lords, who would have used them to accompany solemn rituals or entertain guests. Indeed, in 1978, during the excavation of a huge four-chambered, fifth-century BC tomb at Leigudun in Hubei Province *(pages 47-48)*, an even more magnificent set had come to light. It consisted of 64 bronze bells—ranging in size from eight inches to one five feet tall that weighed 477 pounds—arranged in eight groups according to size and tone, each bell, like those that were displayed in Seattle, with a two-pitch capability. Most had been cast with inscriptions specifying, with remarkable accuracy, their respective notes, indicating that the pitch had been correctly calculated before the bronze bells were cast.

This chime belonged to Marquis Yi, ruler of Zeng, a state that had strong ties to the powerful kingdom of Chu, to the south. The instrument was entombed with him around 433 BC, and incredibly, when the tomb was opened the bells were still in their proper place—hanging mouth down in three rows on a magnificent L-shaped frame comprising lacquered wooden beams supported by six sword-bearing bronze figures. The sturdy frame had supported the bells' nearly three tons for some 2,400 years. Wooden striking implements, discovered not far away, indicated that a number of musicians played the instrument at one time.

The chime was not the only musical instrument that had been entombed with the marquis. Among the some 7,000 artifacts that accompanied him to his grave were 27 drums, zithers, panpipes, mouth organs, and flutes, all typical of a Zhou orchestra. Close by these, the archaeologists came upon further evidence of the marquis's love of music—the remains of 21 young women, some of whom likely were his musicians and dancers. Having charmed the marquis in life, they were apparently sacrificed upon his death so that they might continue to entertain him in the afterlife.

Working ankle-deep in water and mud, archaeologists document their 1978 discovery of the bronze 64-bell chime in Marquis Yi's tomb (right, above). Remarkably well preserved, the instrument (right) required reconstruction of only one lacquered crossbeam before being put on display. When played, the bells on the second row provide the melody line, while larger bells on the bottom produce the accompaniment.

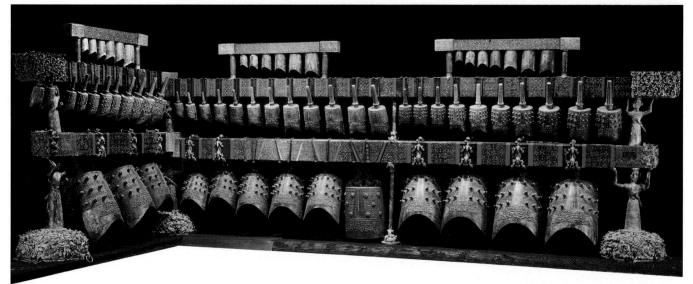

There was also evidence that the marquis was no slouch when it came to military matters: One chamber contained a veritable arsenal of dagger-axes, lances, halberds, spears, bows, arrows, shields, armor, and more than 3,000 bronze arrowheads.

Plainly, the marquis was a man of his time. He lived during the period of the Eastern Zhou (771-221 BC), so named to set it apart from the Western Zhou (c. 1050-771 BC). Historians use 771 as the date dividing the eras, for this was the year that the king moved the capital from the western city of Xi'an to Luoyang in the east to make it safe from barbarians pressing in from the west. The period of the Eastern Zhou can be characterized by the enormous technological, artistic, and intellectual change that took place during its 550-year span, but it was also one of great political instability, constant warfare, and relentless destruction. Scholars estimate that only about one of every five years passed without war, with the result that some 170 Chinese states or principalities fell to the sword as the scale and savagery of the fighting steadily escalated and major powers built up armies a million strong.

Historians split the Eastern Zhou itself into two parts: the Spring and Autumn period, from 771 to 481 BC, and the Warring States period, from 481 to 221 BC. They took their names for these from the titles of two accounts—*Spring and Autumn Annals* and *Discourses of the Warring States*. The former, a laconic chronicle of events in the kingdom of Lu, covers the roughly two and a half centuries prior to 481 BC, when more than a hundred Eastern Zhou states were being swallowed up by more powerful neighbors, until only seven major states and a few lesser kingdoms remained. *Discourses of the Warring States,* a collection of anecdotes and fables, tells of subsequent decades when the seven superstates waged war against one another on a greater scale than ever before.

Most records of the various states were destroyed after the surviving states fell to the Qin. Early in the second century BC, however, a number of scholars began to restore from memory the lost texts and to record events that they had experienced during the troubled years. Most remarkably, Fu Sheng, a Confucian scholar who, though more than 90 years old at the time, dictated to his daughter the memorized text of *The Book of History,* extensive documents from the Western Zhou period.

Among other great works that were somehow preserved is *The Book of Odes,* an anthology of poetry dating from the 10th to the

46

HOUSE OF ETERNITY FOR A MARQUIS, RULER OF THE LOST STATE OF ZENG

The exact location of the state of Zeng, a principality remembered in Chinese history for the alliance it made with two other states to topple the Western Zhou dynasty, eluded scholars for well over a thousand years. Then in 1978, at Leigudun in Hubei Province, archaeologists not only identified Zeng's location, they also came upon a burial of unparalleled richness and complexity.

The enormous tomb *(below),* measuring 68 feet long and 54 feet wide, contained 15,404 relics. Among its treasures were bronze zoomorphic figures and sacrificial vessels of exceptional design; ornamental pieces of jade; bowls, cups, spoons, and buckles of gold; wood and bamboo lacquerware; and an array of weapons and musical instruments.

Inscriptions on the bronzes positively identified the occupant as Zeng Hou Yi, marquis of Zeng, who died in 433 BC. The dating meant that the bamboo slips found in the tomb—slivers of the wood joined by thread—on which ritual prayers and an inventory of burial objects had been noted, were among the oldest examples of their kind. Pictures and descriptions on the lid of a lacquer trunk turned out to be the earliest known Chinese representations of the heavens.

No effort had been spared to surround the marquis of Zeng with the appurtenances of his rank. The four wooden chambers suggested the rooms of a palace. And he was placed in his burial/bedchamber with eight sacrificed female attendants and a dog. A central hall held a complete orchestra of musical instruments, as well as vessels, pots, bowls, and baskets for wine and food, arranged in rows as if for a banquet. A chamber located adjacent to the ceremonial hall contained more sacrifices—13 females between the ages of 15 and 25. Archaeologists suppose that some of them at least were the very musicians who had served their master in life.

The tomb of the marquis consists of four chambers. The room on the right side houses his remains. Stored in the adjacent chamber are musical instruments, while next door stand the caskets of 13 women. The smallest room is an armory. Two coffins encased the silk-clad marquis, the outer made of wood and bronze and the inner (below) of wood alone. Elaborate lacquerwork designs (background, this and following page) covered both coffins.

A cast-gold vessel (right) with a serpentine design encircling both the bowl and the lid formed part of a food and drink set buried with the marquis. The openwork design of the ladle suggests that it was used to strain food from broth.

Dragons writhe and coil on this elaborately decorated bronze wine vessel and basin. Part of the marquis Yi's ceremonial equipment, the piece is one of the earliest known examples of casting with the lost-wax process in ancient China, predating by 200 years the previously assumed date for the method.

A lacquered clothing trunk exhibits a painted representation of the first Chinese astronomical map. The names of 28 constellations surround the word for the Big Dipper; two of four so-called directional animals, the green dragon of the east and the white tiger of the west, flank the cosmic scene.

seventh century BC that evokes the joys and sorrows of life. Later, toward the beginning of the first century BC, came the richest mine of information about the Eastern Zhou era, *Records of the Historian,* an influential work written by the Han court's grand historian, Sima Qian. This history of China recorded major events of the Eastern Zhou and earlier times, supplemented by treatises and chronological charts that aided in understanding these occurrences as well as by biographies of leading figures. In recent decades archaeology has enlarged the written record. The recovery, from myriad tombs, of documents and of artifacts decorated with scenes of war, rituals, and hunting has helped 20th-century scholars fill in missing details.

Despite the upheaval, the approximately 830-year-long line of Zhou kings survived longer than any dynasty in Chinese history. Still, as the kingdom's fortunes changed, the state grew progressively weaker. During the Spring and Autumn period, the power and prestige of the Zhou king declined to the point where his authority was limited to a small territory surrounding Wangcheng, his capital near modern Luoyang in western Henan Province. Beyond this domain he was regarded as no more than a figurehead, still worthy of the title that had been the hereditary right of his forefathers, Son of Heaven, and yet commanding only nominal allegiance from the regions that, between c. 1050 and 771 BC, had once made up the vast realm of the Western Zhou monarchs.

Ranged around the Son of Heaven's diminished kingdom, at the beginning of the Spring and Autumn period, were some 170 individual states, all still linked by tradition to the Zhou ruler. Some occupied large territories; many comprised no more than a fortified town and its adjacent land. Their increasingly independent nature testified to the breakdown of the governmental system built over the years by the Zhou monarchs. For generations the kings had installed their sons and other kinsmen, along with ministers, generals, and trustworthy local rulers, as feudal lords in these lands. In the system's heyday the hereditary dukes, in turn, granted their relatives and ministers parcels of land to assure personal loyalty. The ministers made similar land grants to their subordinates. As an expression of their power, the rulers of the states within the Zhou sphere of influence came to hold various titles—*gong* (duke), *hou* (marquis), *bo* (earl), *zu* (viscount), and *nan* (baron). Inevitably, squabbles broke out among the elite, and court intrigues and power struggles ensued.

Testifying to the benefits that came with being on top of the hierarchy are the magnificent possessions found in the tomb of Marquis Yi of the principality of Zeng. They show that a relatively minor ruler could lead a life of splendor and be held in high esteem. Nonetheless, inscriptions on the bronze objects buried with him suggest that the old system was fast changing; no longer did the Zhou have the upper hand. The marquis may, in fact, have been subordinate to the ruler of the powerful neighboring state of Chu. Indeed, by 433 BC when the marquis died, the lords of Chu had long had the title of *wang*, or king—and in another 100 years so would the rulers of all the other major states.

Throughout the Spring and Autumn period, the number of independent territories steadily declined as the stronger kingdoms overwhelmed and annexed the weaker ones. Rulers, called hegemons or overlords, emerged who were strong enough to assume the leadership of a confederation of states, even while professing to be governing in the name of the Son of Heaven, the Zhou king. Duke Huan of the state of Qi, in Shandong Province, came to power in just such a manner. The duke repelled invading nomads by rallying other states, then he adopted the title of hegemon. In his new capacity, Huan settled disputes between the states and commanded allied forces against barbarian aggressors.

During his long reign (685-643 BC), Huan went to war no fewer than 28 times. He successfully led his allies against the state of Chu to the south, in 656 BC, ostensibly to compel its people to go on paying regular tribute to the Zhou king but more likely to curb Chu's growing power. Evidently Duke Huan regarded such tribute as little more than a formality to be carried out, for it preserved the fiction that the king of Zhou was the Son of Heaven while perpetuating the notion that Duke Huan was one of his close relatives.

Thus the Zhou king retained his ritual function and continued to be consulted by powerful hegemons on matters of ancestry and propriety. Presumably there would come a time when one of them would emerge strong enough to stand alone against all of the others, and Duke Huan envisioned himself as that man and acted accordingly. But it was a dream caught short by his death, after which the state of Qi failed to maintain its domination, and the struggle for the leadership role took on new energy. By the fifth century BC, the major states would abandon much of the pretense of obeisance to a central authority and fight for supremacy among themselves, without a single bow to the Zhou king.

With Zhou power fast crumbling, China's social structure began undergoing radical change. Below the feudal lords was a class called *shi*, or gentlemen, descendants of nobles who were small landlords or served the lords as stewards, minor officials, or professional warriors. By the end of the Spring and Autumn period, however, states had become too large and complex to be dependent on such a small governing class, and some of the shi achieved power as ministers and generals. After the emergence of states in need of more systematic administration, many entered government service to form the backbone of newly established bureaucracies.

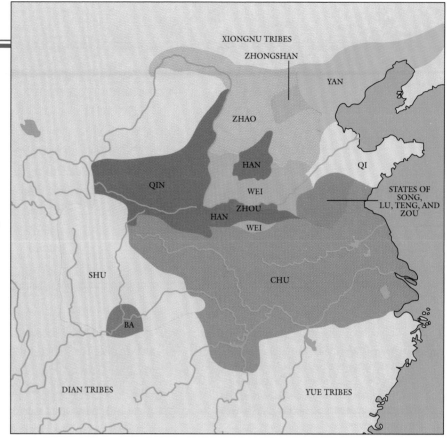

Territorial boundaries changed constantly throughout the volatile Eastern Zhou period. This map approximates the boundaries of the 17 major states or principalities during the fourth and third centuries BC of the aptly named Warring States portion of the era. Qin emerged as victor over all in 221 BC, uniting the smaller principalities into a single political entity.

Military tradition was also changing, if more slowly. For the greater part of the Spring and Autumn period, battles continued to be fought primarily by men of noble descent, who unlike commoners were trained as a matter of course in the skills of swordsmanship, archery, and charioteering. Conscripts drawn from the peasantry played only a minor supporting role as foot soldiers.

The aristocrats observed certain proprieties in the conduct of war. The fighting of a savage, no-holds-barred battle was considered the mark of a barbarian; among the "civilized" Chinese, a battle was seen as a form of gentlemen's duel fought on a large scale, a test of one's honor, character, and skill. The emergence of generals from the ranks of the shi did not dilute this aristocratic approach to war. The shi had always been taught to maintain the proper courtesies in practicing the noble art of combat. Polite exchanges would be made by rival commanders before fighting commenced. For example, it is recorded that a Chu general, in 632 BC, challenged the Qin ruler with the words: "Will Your Excellency permit our knights and yours to play a game?"

For almost two centuries of the Spring and Autumn period, these genteel armies fought mainly with chariots, each drawn by two or four horses and manned by three warriors—a driver and two archers—with perhaps 10 foot soldiers in support. As states became larger and fewer in number, the size of their chariot armies grew. In 589 BC, when the state of Jin went into battle against that of Chi, Jin mounted 800 chariots for a single engagement. The Jin fighting force included 2,400 warriors, plus at least 8,000 foot soldiers.

In recent decades, archaeologists have unearthed the remains of numerous chariots, together with the skeletons of horses, in the burial grounds of Eastern Zhou nobility. Major discoveries were made in the 1930s during excavations of the Wei tombs at Liulige. There the diggers found a pit that contained parts of 19 chariots. Most of the woodwork had decayed, but the metal and bone fittings were still in their original positions, enabling the chariots to be reconstructed with precision.

As the archaeological evidence revealed, Warring States chariots had improved in design, fittings, and mechanical parts. Older chariots had been built with heavy, cumbersome wheels; the newer ones had 26-spoke, bowl-shaped wheels, increasing their resistance to a sideways thrust. The chariots were rendered still more effective by the use of an equine collar harness that did not have a choking effect on the horse. The massed armies of major Zhou states would have presented an awe-inspiring spectacle, with chariots lined up by the hundreds across the battle plain, glittering with bronze fittings of elaborate design. A few of the vehicles had bronze parts decorated with silver and gold and colorful, lacquered woodwork.

Topknotted Dian warriors defeat their pigtailed opponents in battle vignettes depicted on the cover of a bronze container. Scenes on the foot-wide lid reflect the efficacy of new methods of warfare, such as cavalry and the crossbow, developed during the Warring States period. The container was used to hold cowrie shells, a form of currency.

Despite their formidability, chariots were expensive and inefficient and would play a declining role in warfare. By the sixth century BC, military circumstances had begun to dictate changes in fighting techniques. Conflicts moved beyond the crowded but flat central plain and the middle and lower valleys of the Yellow River that had suited chariot warfare. Expanding states increasingly found themselves campaigning over mountainous or marshy terrain totally unsuited to chariots. They needed an entirely new kind of force. Then in the sixth century BC, battles began to be fought by infantry alone. Eventually, all the major states built up battalions of foot soldiers composed almost entirely of conscripted commoners armed with double-edged swords and spears.

The introduction of cavalry, swifter and more mobile than chariots, contributed greatly to military success from the fifth century BC onward. The northern kingdoms, including Qin, Yan, and Zhao, gained in strength by adopting the cavalry tactics of nomadic tribes, together with the dress—tunics, trousers, and pointed riding caps—of the fierce Scythian horsemen of the Eurasian steppes.

During the 290 years of the Spring and Autumn period, no fewer than 110 states were extinguished or annexed. In the aftermath, many nobles lost their aristocratic status. Yet those years were relatively mild compared with the two and a half centuries that followed. The early wars often involved a single major military engagement, which ended quickly in the defeat of one of the parties or a negotiated truce. In the Warring States period, wars became fewer, although 22 states were still being eliminated, but these were conflicts of far greater magnitude and duration. No longer were petty kingdoms in opposition. Now mighty states were so massively armed that fighting often dragged on for years.

It was the increasing use of mass infantry, sometimes supported by mounted archers, that signaled the end of warfare conducted according to polite rules. The demand for foot soldiers opened the way for low-born subjects to break through the old social barriers and rise, for the first time, to positions of authority. Professional warriors advanced rapidly through the ranks. At the same time, aristocrats could be demoted for their incompetence, and many nobles lost all social status following capture in battle. Only results mattered, as states became locked in desperate struggles for survival or supremacy. Those who fought well could gain rich rewards regardless of their social rank. For distinction in battle, shi received tracts of land, commoners official positions, and slaves their freedom.

In some states, men of obscure origin rose to the rank of general. The high value placed on military expertise may be gauged by the experience of Sun Zi, also known as Sun the Cripple. For some unknown misdemeanor, this low-born citizen of Wei suffered the punishment of having his feet lopped off. Subsequently he was recruited by the state of Qi for his skill as a military strategist, and during the Warring States period he rose to become chief of staff.

However much the new social order challenged the basis on which the noble families had held hereditary offices, it tended to strengthen the role of individual lords. In each of the major kingdoms there could now be one ruling house, and its recognized king could promote or demote functionaries however he so desired. Newly captured or colonized land was organized into administrative units that were governed by appointed officials, without hereditary rights. Eventually even hereditary landholdings were reorganized into such administrative units.

Not surprisingly, the lives of the farmers were seriously affected by these changes. Peasants were subject to military conscription, which meant a loss of their labor to their families, who would also have to cover the cost of outfitting the men for the army. Those who stayed behind to work the land suffered constantly from the heavy taxes imposed to pay for the wars and the building of walls, highways, and canals. The old feudal system had offered a modicum of security: If the farmer fulfilled his obligations to his lord in good times, he was not thrown off the land in the bad years. A peasant could now lose his land if he failed to pay his taxes and often had to take out high-interest loans to make ends meet.

As the scale of warfare steadily mounted, battles might be fought continuously for more than a week, and the siege of a city could last for months. There are no statistics relating to the total number of casualties sustained in the years of the Warring States period. But it is believed that millions of Chinese were killed since armies began to abandon the practice of taking prisoners of war, choosing instead to meet resistance with wholesale slaughter. For example, *Records of the Historian* notes that after Qin forces overwhelmed the army of the state of Zhao in the campaign of Changping in 260 BC, some 450,000 captured soldiers were executed and buried in mass graves by their vanquishers.

Evidence of a massacre on this scale has not yet turned up,

although a Chinese archaeologist has suggested that one grave dating from the period may have been uncovered in the 1930s, when workers were excavating Wei tombs at Liulige, in the district of modern Huixian. There they came across a shallow trench containing some 60 bodies, all of which had been decapitated; a few arrowheads lodged in several ribs suggested that the victims had been captives who had been buried en masse.

For all its horrors, war provided a powerful impetus to new enterprises. During the Spring and Autumn period, defensive needs were met by the construction of higher and stronger city walls and watchtowers. Such walls were frequently built by ramming dry earth or clay into large wooden frames, which were removed once the tamped earth was compacted solid; impressions left by the frames still attest to this method. At Dan, capital of a state of the same name that was subjugated by Qi in 684 BC, excavations revealed that a shallow trench had been dug and then filled up with layers of tamped earth to serve as a foundation for a wall; the barrier itself, some 12 yards thick at its base, was constructed of ever rising layers of tamped earth mixed with a quantity of stone. Each new layer sloped slightly so that the wall would taper.

By the late Spring and Autumn period, many cities had grown so large that they were provided with a second, outer wall of defense. Similarly, territorial expansion prompted the larger states to begin building so-called *changcheng,* or long walls, to defend their new frontiers. Chu and Qi initiated this strategy, and remains of Qi's longest wall can still be seen along its entire length of about 260 miles, stretching from the south bank of the Yellow River to the eastern seaboard at Jiaonan. Later, as nomads threatened great northern states, more sophisticated methods were used to build defensive walls extending over hilly terrain. Investigation of the remains of the outer wall of Yan, a northeastern state located in what is today's Hebei and Liaoning provinces, has shown that the sections in mountainous areas were constructed of blocks of stone, with watchtowers spaced at regular intervals so guards could signal to one another.

For more effective warfare, weapons underwent massive change. Traditional arms—dagger-axes, halberds, spears, knives, bows, and arrows—were constantly redesigned or modified for greater effectiveness. And for the first time swords came into large-

RESPECTFUL GREETINGS FROM LONG, LONG AGO

Remnants of the burial mound and of storage pits flank the burial chamber of King Cuo. Zhongshan's conquerors probably opened and pillaged the tomb just a few years after it was built.

In the mid-1940s a Hebei Province farmer, Liu Ximei, came upon a worn stone inscribed with strange characters. Intrigued, he removed the 2½- by 3-foot granite slab from the stream bed where it lay and carried it home to keep under the eaves of his house. Thirty-five years later he produced the curious relic for archaeologists working in the area. As it turned out, the characters on the River-Polished Stone, so-called for the smooth surface and rounded edges it acquired from centuries of erosion by the currents, dated from the Warring States period (481-221 BC). This made it one of the oldest such monuments in the history of ancient China. Translation of its two-line inscription—"Royal fishpond watcher Gongcheng De and tomb overseer Jiujiang Man respectfully greet gentlemen of the future generations"—confirmed long-held suspicions that local tombs belonged to Warring States nobility.

Subsequent excavation of 30 of these burial places not only revealed that they indeed dated from the Warring States period but also conclusively established the area as site of Lingshou, capital of the Zhongshan Kingdom. More than 2,000 bronze objects emerged from the dig, 90 of which bore inscriptions ranging from lists of kings to advice for future generations on the handling of foreign affairs.

Founded in 414 BC by a northern ethnic group known as Baidi, or White Di, Zhongshan figured prominently in the power struggles of the day. The once nomadic Di settled in the central plain and came to dominate its farming and industrial society. Their kingdom prospered and eventually became known as the "state of a thousand chariots."

One of the tombs explored belonged to King Cuo, ruler of Zhongshan from 323 to 311 BC. The excavation revealed that he

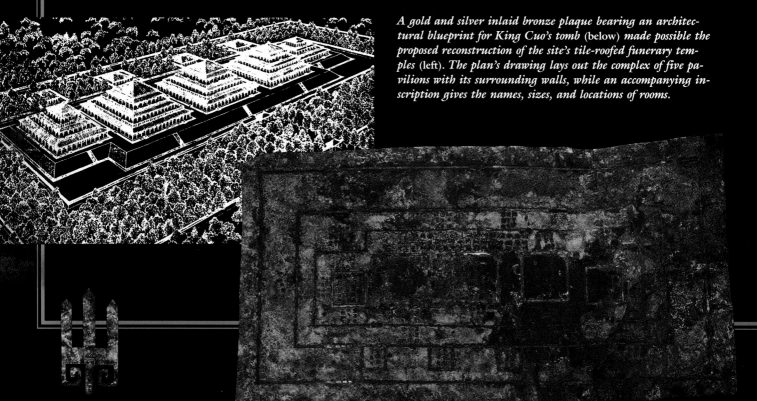

A gold and silver inlaid bronze plaque bearing an architectural blueprint for King Cuo's tomb (below) made possible the proposed reconstruction of the site's tile-roofed funerary temples (left). The plan's drawing lays out the complex of five pavilions with its surrounding walls, while an accompanying inscription gives the names, sizes, and locations of rooms.

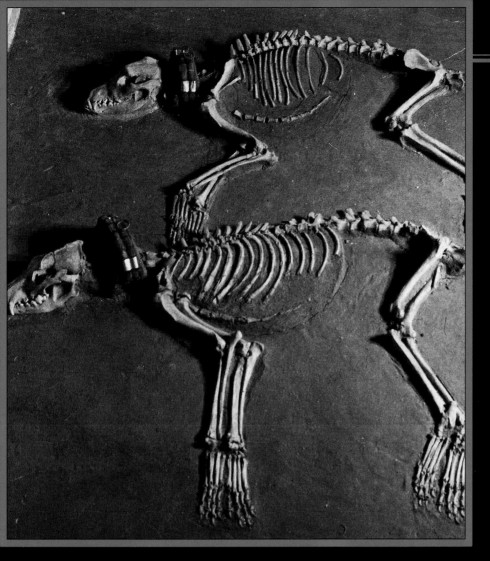

Heavy gold and silver collars adorn the skeletal remains of two large wolflike "north dogs," a breed used for hunting by the Di. Found alongside a chariot and horses in King Cuo's tomb, the dogs completed an assemblage of items necessary for the pursuit of game, presumably an activity the ruler had enjoyed in life.

Bronze insignia in the shape of the Chinese character shan, or mountain, lie as found near the king's tomb. Placed atop wooden poles, the 56-inch-high symbols were probably used in front of the palace or on the royal chariot.

had gone to his rest accompanied by two queens and several retainers, horses, chariots, and boats. Over the tomb had stretched a 120-yard-long mound, surmounted by stepped funerary temples *(far left)*. Although plundered long ago, Cou's sepulcher yielded many historically valuable articles. One was a bronze plate incised with the architectural design for the complex. The drawing, while inaccurate in scale, provides precise measurements of the 2,300-year-old funerary monument.

Although the Di merged with the people of the central plain, they retained many unique remnants of their nomadic past. Emblems in the shape of a trident, perhaps the symbol for mountain, abound on tools, bronzes, and ceramics. Traditionally, the Di venerated the mountains to the west as their place of origin and as a bulwark against enemies. The barrier proved to be no match for the hegemonic ambitions of the neighboring state of Zhao, which conquered Zhongshan in 296 BC.

scale production. Swords were not widely used in China before the Zhou dynasty; and the few made were usually cast of bronze in one piece without an integral hilt. But by the seventh century BC, they were given proper handles of wood or ivory, bound with woven silk or cord to strengthen the grip, often with a guard between the hilt and the blade. Swords found in later Zhou tombs were often enhanced by jade fittings as well as by silver and gold inlay. Some had a guard made of jade and were housed in a scabbard of lacquered bamboo, leather, or ivory.

The age-old dagger-ax, commonly carried by infantry and charioteers, also was redesigned. As depicted in battles scenes on bronze vessels, dagger-axes now came in three sizes: The longest one, measuring about twice the height of a warrior, was designed for attacking chariots and boats, while shorter versions were used in hand-to-hand combat. In a further deadly refinement, the multipurpose dagger-ax was fitted with a hook-shaped blade on the lower end of the handle. The weapon could thus be used in all directions—stabbing forward, scything to the left or right, or thrusting backward to ward off an attack from the rear.

To this lethal arsenal was added the crossbow (page 52), which became a standard weapon in the fifth century BC, some 13 centuries before it was introduced into Europe. As shown by reconstructions based on surviving parts, the Eastern Zhou crossbow comprised a wooden stock with a grip, a bow of laminated bamboo, and a trigger mechanism of bronze cast in four parts. The crossbow was placed under tension with the foot; it fired small metal-tipped bolts at such great velocity that it soon became recognized as the deadliest weapon in the whole Zhou arsenal.

As military forces became better equipped, the demand for mineral and agricultural supplies necessary to sustain ever-larger armies grew. Economic strength was recognized as being every bit as important as military might. Accordingly, great technological advances were made in the exploitation of natural wealth.

Early in the Warring States period, the Chinese commenced using iron on a greater scale. There is some evidence that small amounts of iron were worked as early as the 11th century BC during the Shang dynastic period, but it had long been considered an ugly metal by the bronze-loving nobility. Some scholars believe that a shortage of copper and tin, the ingredients of bronze, prompted the Zhou to begin casting iron in significant volume in the sixth century

BC. They already possessed the technology, including highly efficient kilns and bellows used to produce bronzes, that allowed them to achieve the extremely high temperature—about 2,800 degrees Fahrenheit—required to smelt the iron ore. The slag could then be skimmed from the top and the molten iron poured into a mold. In the West, the process of casting iron would not be widely practiced until some 1,800 years later.

During recent decades, excavations have brought to light hundreds of cast-iron implements from many kingdoms. In 1965, at the Yan capital of Xiadu in Hebei Province, a late Warring States tomb yielded not only scores of iron weapons but also iron armor, consisting of 89 interlinking plates. Finds from this and other graves show that high carbon steel was also being manufactured at this time—although in less quantity—and used in spears and halberds.

Even more important than the weapons of war was iron's impact on farming. The remains of factory sites and numerous tools suggest that, increasingly, by the fourth century BC, iron was being cast into plowshares, hoes, picks, spades, rakes, sickles, and axes. In 1954 the ruins of a Yan workshop at Xinglong, in Hebei Province,

A bronze vessel containing wine that turned green from minerals leached from its container lay in the treasury in the tomb of Zhongshan's King Cuo for 2,300 years. Analysis of the fragrant liquid (in beaker, right) *revealed a toddylike beverage consisting of alcohol, sugar, and fat.*

were examined. The factory, built near two iron mines, occupied an area of nearly 36,000 square yards and contained 48 sets of molds that had been utilized primarily for the production of iron farm implements. The casting of iron in large foundries under state control was moving the Chinese a step closer to mass production.

Being more brittle than bronze, iron was not necessarily an improvement. But because of the metal's comparative cheapness, tools manufactured at factories such as the Yan workshop could be made available to the peasants, many of whom were still relying on primitive wood, stone, or shell tools. Consequently, work on the land became somewhat easier, and farmers could clear and cultivate more acreage and achieve deeper furrowing during spring plowing. The result contributed to a marked increase in agricultural output.

Flooding, so destructive to crops and fields, was reduced by the construction of numerous dams, dikes, and canals. These, in turn, brought controlled irrigation to large tracts of previously unusable land. Such projects frequently sprang from military necessity. In 486 BC, for example, the prince of Wu ordered the construction of a waterway linking the Huai and Yangzi rivers, in order to provide a direct supply route for his army as it marched on the northern states of Song and Lu. The result was the nearly 100-mile-long Han Gou Canal, which today makes up a section of the Grand Canal between Hangzhou and Beijing.

By around 250 BC hydraulic engineering had developed into an advanced science, as evinced by the works of Li Bing, appointed governor of the Qin commandery, or military province, of the state of Shu in that year. Li Bing built an irrigation network that brought great prosperity to the Chengdu region. There, by cutting a gorge some 130 feet deep through solid rock, he diverted the Min River and controlled its flow with an intricate system of dams, canals, and locks that made extensive agriculture possible on the entire Chengdu Plain, which encompassed an area of some 6,200 square miles. Li Bing's scheme was so soundly designed that a portion of it still operates in modern Sichuan, although in a somewhat modified form after more than 2,000 years.

According to *Records of the Historian,* a similar beneficial project, undertaken around the same time, originated because of political intrigue: The prince of Han had the idea of countering the eastward expansion of Qin by exhausting that state with ambitious engineering projects. To this end, he dispatched a waterworks specialist, Zheng Guo, to persuade the Qin ruler to dig a canal joining the Ching and Lo rivers. The waterway was half finished when the Qin prince learned of the ploy. But Zheng Guo was so convincing in arguing the merits of the scheme that he was allowed to continue.

When the canal was opened in 246 BC, it rapidly transformed what is now central Shaanxi into a key economic area. The irrigation system led to a fivefold increase in production, while the channel itself provided a water route for shipping huge quantities of grain into the heart of the burgeoning Qin state.

Such large-scale engineering projects had profound social effects that went beyond their immediate aim of supporting great armies. As might be expected, increased food production led to population growth. Although no census was conducted at the time, later statistics suggest that during the Eastern Zhou the population of China may have swelled from about 10 million to roughly 50 million. This rise was accompanied by the development of great cities that began as military strongholds and became commercially significant.

Gold and silver threads and inlays adorn a vividly realistic, yet stylized, Zhongshan bronze of a tiger in the act of devouring a fawn. A spectacular example of artisanship, the crouching beast probably acted as the base for a piece of furniture whose wooden frame decayed long ago.

Cities of about 100,000 were common throughout China in the Warring States period, and there were some with even larger populations. The Qi capital of Linzi in northeast Shandong Province reportedly had about 350,000 citizens in the fourth century BC. Near the end of the next century, the Zhou capital of Wangcheng, not far from present-day Luoyang, is said to have had more than a quarter of a million inhabitants.

Curiously, centuries of bitter conflict did not lead to drastic reduction in civilian movement and trade; in fact, travel and commerce increased, often aided by roads and waterways improved for military traffic. When states were not actually fighting one another, they were competing fiercely to attract the most talented officials, technicians, and scholars, as well as to import minerals and goods not readily available in their own lands. Such high value was placed on trade that even kingdoms at war reached agreements that allowed

merchants to cross disputed frontiers. Moreover, as the number of states dwindled, the triumphant powers were able to assure safe passage throughout the larger territories under their control, which meant that merchants, technicians, and scholars could travel more expeditiously between capitals. An ever greater exchange of goods, production techniques, and ideas took place, and a growing sense of cultural unity began to emerge among the peoples of the Chinese states, one that would eventually transcend regional differences.

Urban areas became thriving manufacturing centers, with factories turning out everything from bronze objects to fabrics. The massive scale of production is indicated by findings at scores of archaeological digs, as at the site of the Zhou capital at Luoyang. There 8,000 pieces of stone, including carvings and jade objects of the Warring States period, were uncovered, all apparently from one major workshop. At Houma, a major city of the state of Jin in Shanxi Province, remains of a bronze foundry included more than 30,000 earthenware molds and tens of thousands of fragments of crucibles and other molds for casting tools, vessels, weapons, and coins.

Continuing a tradition established in Shang times, Eastern Zhou artisans cast bronze objects of extraordinary complexity and exquisite decoration. Sometime around 550 BC, they began to use the lost-wax process, a means of creating individual works of intricate detail not possible with the traditional section-mold method. For the lost-wax technique, they created a model from wax and carved and engraved details into it. They then applied wet clay to completely cover the model to form a mold, leaving small holes in the mold. Next, they fired the mold, which allowed the wax to melt and run out or burn off through the holes. Pouring molten bronze into the space in the mold where the wax had been, they cast an object that had the same shape and details of the model but one with all the permanence that the original lacked.

Artisans also achieved a relatively high level of technology in the production of gold and silver artifacts, including vessels for eating and drinking, necklaces, ear pendants, belt buckles, and ornaments shaped as humans, birds, and animals. Luxury items, these belonged to high-ranking personages, and very few have been found. For aristocratic men and women, jade was the natural choice when fashioned into necklaces, hairpins, belt ornaments, and pendants of birds, animals, or geometric designs. The production of such items, however small they may have been, involved long hours of intensive

Embroidered dragons, tigers, and phoenixes embellish the woven gauze of a 2,300-year-old silk robe. Remarkably well preserved, the cache of 35 silk garments and quilted robes found in a Chu kingdom tomb reveals much about the high levels of both textile technology and handwork of the Warring States period.

COMMUNICATIONS ACROSS THE CENTURIES: CHINA'S AGELESS WRITTEN LANGUAGE

Chinese tradition maintains that the ability to read and to write epitomizes erudition in much the same way that Greeks and Romans revered oratorical skill. Indeed, the Chinese word *wen* can mean either "civilization" or "text."

Although mastery of the complex writing system is daunting, taking an average of 10 years even for native speakers, the cultural rewards are many, for with mastery comes access to every great classical text of the Chinese past. Astonishingly, Chinese script has changed so little in 2,500 years that it is no more difficult to read Confucius than to read modern poetry written in the classical style.

The standardization of the script evolved from a need for communication among the many segments of the far-flung Chinese world. Because the written characters are logographs, carrying meaning rather than sound, the reader need not speak the same dialect as the writer. This feature was imperative because, at any given time, the number of Chinese spoken dialects ranged from 20 to more than 100. In fact, modern readers of ancient texts often are completely unaware of the pronunciation that was used by early authors.

The origin of Chinese writing is obscure. The earliest known diagrammatic signs appear on Neolithic pottery carbon-dated to 5000 or 4000 BC. These forerunners of what is certainly one of the world's oldest written languages display

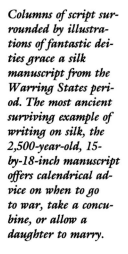

Columns of script surrounded by illustrations of fantastic deities grace a silk manuscript from the Warring States period. The most ancient surviving example of writing on silk, the 2,500-year-old, 15-by-18-inch manuscript offers calendrical advice on when to go to war, take a concubine, or allow a daughter to marry.

kinship to subsequent characters inscribed on oracle bones and bronze vessels from the Shang and Zhou dynasties. Although these examples are several centuries apart in age, inscription of the characters with a hard stylus produced a similar angularity of form. Later on, with the widespread use of brush and ink on bamboo, wood, and silk during the Eastern Zhou period, the script took on more flowing lines. The evolving graph for fish, illustrated at upper left, exemplifies how the medium affected the message.

The rulers of the third-century BC Qin dynasty established the most sweeping reforms in the written language, making the characters absolutely standardized in the drive to centralize the power of the state. With some minor changes, it is this version that survives to the present day.

The development of the script depended, in part, upon its function. The archaic writing, used for divinations (oracle bones), king lists, and tomb inventories, grew to accommodate more difficult concepts. The symbols became compounds, consisting of a logograph and a modifier or two logographs in juxtaposition. For example, the characters for "woman" and "child" are combined to mean "good" or "likable." Today, a new concept such as "laser" becomes "stimulate-light-tube." In this fashion, the lexicon of Chinese characters expanded from about 2,500 in archaic times to more than 50,000 in modern dictionaries.

Although only about 5,000 characters are really necessary for literacy, reformers complain about the lack of accessibility for most people. Attempts to simplify the script have been instituted, and, after thousands of years, these appear to threaten the Confucian ideal that "all under heaven, the carriages have the same track, the books are in the same script, and behavior follows the same ethics."

Scales and weights, a brush, ink, and blank bamboo slips for writing fill what may have been a writing kit. The two-and-a-half-millennia-old brush, the oldest found thus far, consists of rabbit hair bound to a wooden shaft with thread and lacquer.

A text from 400-300 BC contains the earliest known tables of multiplication and division. The problems worked out here are the familiar 2x9 = 18 and 3x9 = 27.

Beautifully executed characters covered bamboo slips such as these found in a Western Han tomb in Shandong Province. The slips contain questions and answers pertaining to the art of war. Although some specific strategies are offered, the speaker concludes that prevention of war is preferable and that "always abiding by promises makes a prosperous kingdom."

labor. The interlocked crystals of jade made it impossible for the artisans to carve the stone with ordinary tools; they had to wear it away and employed an abrasive such as powdered quartz or crushed garnets to make this possible.

The art of lacquering had been practiced during the Shang and Western Zhou years. During the Eastern Zhou period, it was used more extensively, and the skill was further advanced. Lacquer was applied to wood and metal and even used on leather. Shields, for example, were produced by stretching leather on a frame and strengthening it with layers of the resin. Complex designs based on motifs such as dragons or clouds would then be painted on the shields with colored lacquer in black, yellow, brown, and red.

From several excavations have come silk fabrics to demonstrate just how advanced the techniques of spinning and weaving had become during the Eastern Zhou. Surviving examples are embroidered and brocaded with a variety of decorative patterns that include mythological creatures such as dragons and phoenixes as well as interlocked squares and diverse geometric designs. That any silk survives at all from this period can seem a miracle. In January 1982 archaeologists unearthing a small Chu tomb on the site of a brick and tile factory at Mashan, in the northwest of present-day Jiangling County, opened a coffin and found the remains of a woman wrapped in 13 layers of rich silk garments and multicolored quilts with complex designs, fastened with nine silk ribbons. The woman had been clothed in a lined coat, brocade trousers, a skirt, and two brocade robes; her face was covered with a trapezoid silk handkerchief. Silk ribbons had been tied around her thumbs and arms.

Although used primarily for apparel and household items such as quilts and bags, silk was sometimes employed as a writing material. It had the advantage of being lightweight and could be easily rolled up for carrying. However, it was not only perishable but also too expensive to be widely employed. Consequently, only one inscribed silk from the period has been found to date—a manuscript said to have been plundered around 1940 from a Chu tomb at Zidanku, in Changsha, Hunan Province, and subsequently housed in a private collection (page 63).

Just as warfare and the resulting consolidation of power encouraged technological development, so it stimulated intellectual activity. Scholars turned to philosophy to reexamine the nature of humanity,

ONE HUNDRED SCHOOLS OF THOUGHT

In spite of incessant warfare and social and political turmoil, the Eastern Zhou period was one of the most dynamic and intellectually constructive eras in human history. Over the years, competing philosophies proliferated, a phenomenon characterized as the Hundred Schools of Thought.

The most renowned of the great Zhou philosophers was born Kong Zi and subsequently given the title Kong Fuzi (Master Kong), later Latinized by Jesuit missionaries in the 17th century to Confucius. In response to the social upheaval and moral decline of his era, Confucius sought to discover ways of achieving a well-disciplined social order. Largely self-educated, Confucius took his inspiration from ancient Chinese literature, culling the best of early Zhou traditions—most notably respect for authority and veneration of elders and ancestors. Propriety and a sense of duty were fundamental to his teachings. "The gentleman," the philosopher stated, "makes demands on himself; the inferior man makes demands on others."

A pragmatist, Confucius aspired to public office in order to implement his teachings. At the age of 50 or so, he gained a position as minister in his native state of Lu. His virtuous tenure resulted in such an extraordinary reduction in crime that it was said a purse dropped in the street would lie untouched for days. Political intrigue eventually drove him from office, and Confucius devoted his last years to teaching and writing.

The Analects, a posthumous collection of the philosopher's sayings, provides the best evidence of Confucius's teachings. Here emerges a system of ethics, politics, and personal conduct, set out as a blueprint that if followed will be to the ultimate good of both the individual and society.

Daoism, another major Zhou philosophy, also came about as a reaction to the unsettling times. Later legend had it that its founder, Lao Zi, was carried in his mother's womb for 62 years and was born as a white-haired old man. The volume attributed to Lao Zi—*Daodejing (The Way and Its Power)*—reflects the Daoist philosophy of *wu wei,* which is defined as "doing everything by doing nothing" or a minimum of societal rules and regulations. The *Daodejing* is the most frequently translated Chinese book, and it appears in numerous foreign languages around the world 5,000 years after its conception.

searching for new formulas for a peaceful, well-ordered society. Rulers felt the need to seek out thinkers with fresh ideas not only for improving military and economic strategy but also for establishing a more stable and efficient society. They were also seeking a philosophical basis to justify their actions, which they hoped would be seen as promoting the welfare of the people. Under their patronage, Chinese philosophy prospered. King Xuan of Qi, for example, in the late fourth century BC, conducted his patronage on a grand scale, inviting about a thousand learned men from territories under his rule to take up residence in his capital. No demands were placed on his honored guests; they could remain indefinitely to discuss philosophical questions at their leisure.

The new breed of scholars was drawn primarily from the ranks of the shi. Many of them roamed from one state to another, to offer their services to any lord who was willing to listen to their ideas. Schools of philosophy emerged, some of them focusing on metaphysical problems such as defining the meaning of life. But most Eastern Zhou philosophers, responding to a popular craving for peace, tried to formulate the ethics, politics, and economics necessary for creating and maintaining an ideal society. Among these scholars was Confucius (551 to 479 BC), today the most widely known philosopher of the age. A later follower of Confucius, Xunzi (c. 298-230 BC), contended that the inherently evil nature of human beings could and should be reformed through classical education, moral training, and strict adherence to the rules set down by society. Deploring the corruption and violence of his time, Xunzi argued that natural human desires need to be guided and restrained by strict rules of propriety and that character must be shaped by the well-ordered observance of rites.

Xunzi's disciples included several scholars who eventually became leading advocates of a school of philosophy often called Legalism. For these thinkers, it was not enough to rely on education in pursuit of propriety; human behavior must be controlled by strictly imposed laws, with severe punishments for transgressions and rewards for compliance. Still more radically, Legalists elevated a new principle to top priority—unswerving loyalty to the ruler of the state. They rejected Confucian ethics, which were principles to which even monarchs must adhere. In-

CONFUCIUS

stead, Legalists espoused the belief that whatever contributed to the state's power and orderliness should be deemed right, and they demanded absolute obedience to central authority. Furthermore, they advocated a total commitment to the production of food and the buildup of military might in order to ensure a well-fed and acquiescent population. By this means, they argued, the state would become powerful enough to overcome all opposition and unify China, ending the chaos and bringing about a rule of law and order.

Here was a radical school of philosophy that appealed to ruling princes, and it was wholeheartedly embraced by the state of Qin following the arrival, in 361 BC, of the Legalist Shang Yang. Previously, Shang Yang had been a government official in Wei, Qin's traditional enemy. But now, unable to achieve sufficient rank, he switched his allegiance in response to an appeal by the newly installed Qin ruler, Duke Xiao, for someone to assist him in recovering territory that had been lost to Wei a few years earlier.

Shang Yang rapidly gained promotion after impressing Xiao with his ideas of ruthless government and served as chancellor from 359 to 338 BC. Under his direction, draconian measures were introduced to direct all the energies and resources of the kingdom to the dual purposes of increasing agricultural production and waging war. As a result, virtually all the males among the common people were organized into well-trained soldier-farmers, who could be called upon when needed for military service.

Throughout the reign of Xiao, Shang Yang succeeded in his efforts to sustain large armies; he was also a victorious military commander against Wei. But when Xiao died in 338 BC, the most powerful of Legalists was doomed. Years earlier Shang Yang had incurred the displeasure of the heir apparent; following the succession, he was promptly charged with treason. Shang Yang met his death in battle after an unsuccessful attempt to flee; as a posthumous punishment, his body was fastened to two chariots and pulled apart as their horses galloped off in opposite directions.

After nearly a century of conflict in the Warring States period, there remained in 403 BC—besides a few minor principalities—only seven major independent kingdoms: Han, Wei, and Zhao, three central states that had been created toward the end of the fifth century BC by the partition of the kingdom of Jin in today's Shanxi, Hebei, and Henan provinces; the rich and ancient kingdom of Qi on the Shandong peninsula in the northeast; Yan, with its capital near present-day Beijing; and the two greatest powers, Chu and Qin.

Chu, a central southern kingdom occupying the valleys of the middle Yangzi and Han rivers, devoured more than 40 states in the Spring and Autumn period, emerging as the strongest power in South China by the sixth century BC. Numerous Chu tombs, filled with sumptuous artifacts of superior craftsmanship, attest to its wealth. In Henan Province alone, more than 2,000 Chu tombs have been excavated, and large numbers also have been found in Hubei and Hunan provinces. These have yielded not only a wealth of exquisite bronzes, lacquered objects, and jade ornaments but also rare silk fabrics, silk paintings, and bamboo manuscripts, and, in one instance, an urn containing 392 gold coins.

Remembered for its victories, Chu also became famous for intellectual endeavor. Among its most celebrated literary figures was Qu Yuan, a poet who functioned as a leading government minister toward the end of the Warring States period, at a time when Chu was a power rivaled only by Qin. Rightly he warned his monarch against diplomatic negotiations with Qin. Other sages had expressed similar reservations. "Appeasing Qin by giving her territory is like putting out a fire with kindling," cautioned an ancient saying.

Qu Yuan's protests were in vain, however, and he was dismissed from office. In exile, he wrote his best-known poem, *On Encountering Sorrow,* which included the lines: "How well I know that loyalty brings disaster. Yet I will endure; I cannot give up." But Qu Yuan did give up. He was so disenchanted that he committed suicide by jumping into the Miluo River, an event commemorated to this day by China's annual Dragon Boat Festival.

Both Chu and the state of Qin had traditionally been regarded by the central kingdoms as semibarbarian lands beyond the Chinese cultural area. Qin lay astride the main trade routes between China and Central Asia. In 771 BC the Zhou king had called upon the Qin lord for assistance during the historic barbarian assault that had forced the king to move his capital east to Luoyang for safety. Qin forces successfully covered the famed withdrawal, and in gratitude, the king granted Qin a large area of land in the fertile Wei valley, in Shaanxi Province. With the land allotment came new status for the principality. Qin's expansion thereafter would be relentless. By the second half of the fourth century BC, it had become the most powerful kingdom in China.

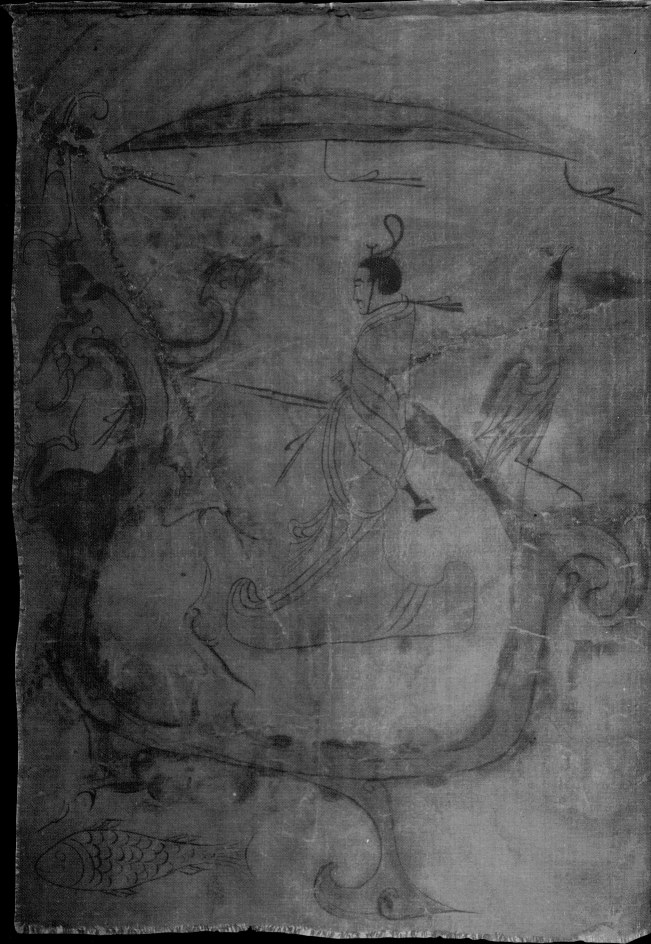

Perhaps Qin's rise owed most to the fact that it had developed under the constant threat of raids by nomadic horsemen from the west. In response, Qin had built up its own highly efficient cavalry and an energetic, centralized government, modeled after the military. But it was its mass infantry that made the crucial difference. Both Chu and Qin eventually had a million conscripted foot soldiers under arms, and these were used on such a scale that battle lines sometimes extended hundreds of miles.

For a short time, a defensive alliance of the other six states of China halted Qin's eastward advance. Unhappily for these states, the alliance lasted only 15 years, for while all six feared Qin, they hated one another even more. According to *Stratagems of the Warring States,* each made the fatal error of trying to appease Qin by bribery so that it would not enter into war on the enemy's side. Divided, the six states were doomed to fall.

The Warring States period entered its last cataclysmic stage in 256 BC, as Qin armies swept across China's vast central plain, overrunning the much shrunken kingdom of Zhou and so bringing to an end the nominal rule of the Zhou dynasty. Then the army drove south, north, and east to conquer one great state after another. The old, feudal world of the Eastern Zhou was destroyed. For the first time, one ruling house commanded the entire Chinese world, stretching from the Yangzi River valley to the northern steppes and from the borders of Central Asia to the East China Sea. The future was already at hand; a unified China would emerge quite soon, founded on a thriving agricultural and industrial base and endowed with a distinct Chinese culture.

CHINA'S DESERT TIME CAPSULE

One of the world's most remarkable archaeological regions is little known and infrequently visited. Its remoteness in northwestern China has largely seen to that. Yet its discovery dates back to the beginning of the 20th century, when Swedish explorer and geographer Sven Hedin and a crew of five on a surveying and mapping expedition of the vast, treacherous Taklamakan Desert stumbled upon desolate ruins. These were enough to convince Hedin that tales of lost cities and buried treasure in the area might be true, and in the days ahead he made a point of investigating the sand-filled buildings his party came upon.

On the afternoon of March 28, 1900, Hedin sighted remnants of wooden houses perched on a nine-foot-high, partially eroded mound. The men searched the dwellings, uncovered a few ancient Chinese coins and tools, and in their haste to return to base camp, left the party's only spade behind. Hedin sent his assistant back for the valuable item. Arriving at the ruins, the man found that a violent sandstorm had come and gone and exposed a large citadel of sun-dried bricks. And thus came to light the stronghold of Loulan, a once thriving oasis community, buried in sand for 1,500 years.

Loulan was but one of the many prosperous Taklamakan caravan stops and trading centers on the Silk Road. During its heyday, the area boasted a post office, a hospital, schools, and a centralized government. But while reaching a zenith of prosperity during the Han dynasty and the two centuries that followed it, Loulan and other oasis towns and settlements turned out to possess a much longer history than Hedin could have dreamed of. Neolithic tools and utensils unearthed in the desert's Lop Nor region show that hunter-gatherers lived there as far back as 8000 BC, when the climate was more salubrious than it is today. Other evidence from the Taklamakan tracks the development of the region through the Bronze Age well into historical times.

Although the Taklamakan hosted thousands of years of human habitation, life could only have become harder and harder as the aridity of the area steadily increased. The desert's Turkic name, meaning "go in and you won't come out," sums up the memories of many who traveled there. Hedin considered it "the worst and most dangerous desert in the world," and tales abound of entire caravans being swallowed up by what a British diplomat called the "giant waves of a petrified ocean"—drifting sand dunes as high as 300 feet.

Ironically, the magnificent preservation of artifacts from the Taklamakan is the result of the same harsh climatic conditions that snuffed out individuals and villages alike. The desert sand acted as a desiccant, causing buried bodies to mummify so completely that every physical feature remained intact *(below)*. Burial goods, such as fabrics, wooden implements, and basketry that would have decomposed elsewhere also were preserved. Perhaps the most important finds were documents, many found by British explorer Aurel Stein in the early 1900s. Written on wooden tablets and paper in Chinese and Indian scripts, the nearly 1,500- to 1,700-year-old letters and legal records give voice to the otherwise mute past, imbuing it with a personal dimension even the most intimate of artifacts cannot provide.

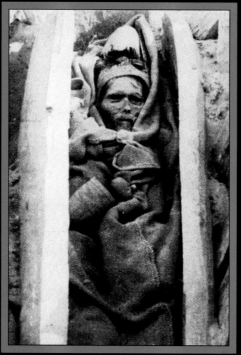

Enclosed within its hollowed-out poplar coffin, the shrouded, mummified corpse of a young male unearthed by explorer Aurel Stein in 1915 exemplifies the excellent state of desert burials. Stein wrote, "The skin all over the body stuck close to the bones, and the odor rising from the body was still pungent."

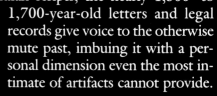

Loulan citadel was painstakingly excavated by a Chinese archaeological team in 1980. Aerial surveys revealed that the fortress had once stood on an island situated between two branches of a long-vanished river.

LIFE AND DEATH AT THE FRINGE

Like buried time capsules, graves on the periphery of the Taklamakan and Lop deserts, some of them 4,000 years old, contained fascinating vestiges of the ancient inhabitants' daily lives—everything from woolen blankets, sheepskin clothing, and leather shoes to wooden vessels and woven-grass baskets. But the so-called Sacred Circle and Kongque River burial barrow, 42 groups of tombs excavated in 1979, revealed a belief system as well; the presence there of kernels of wheat and goddesslike figurines suggested a developed concern with the afterlife. The graves themselves exhibited an east-west orientation, and the bodies were laid out in a careful and consistent manner.

The homely nature of the burial goods attests to the fact that the people of the desert had to struggle for their survival. For a long time, though, they faced each challenge before them with resourcefulness and ingenuity. Hunting and gathering gave way to agriculture and an increasing reliance on animal husbandry. Later, large-scale irrigation systems made the most of the limited water supply, the glacier-fed streams and rivers that originated in the surrounding mountain ranges. Encroachment by the desert was relentless, however, and shrinking glaciers caused even the most verdant of oases to dry up, with the result that entire towns were abandoned and soon swallowed by the sand.

Concentric rings of wooden stakes encircle the tomb of six males buried on the north bank of the now-dry Kongque River.

Additional stakes radiate outward from the Sacred Circle in rows marking the four cardinal directions.

Smooth stones of variegated shale, found clasped in the hands of many of the deceased at Kongque, may have served as talismans for the journey into the afterlife.

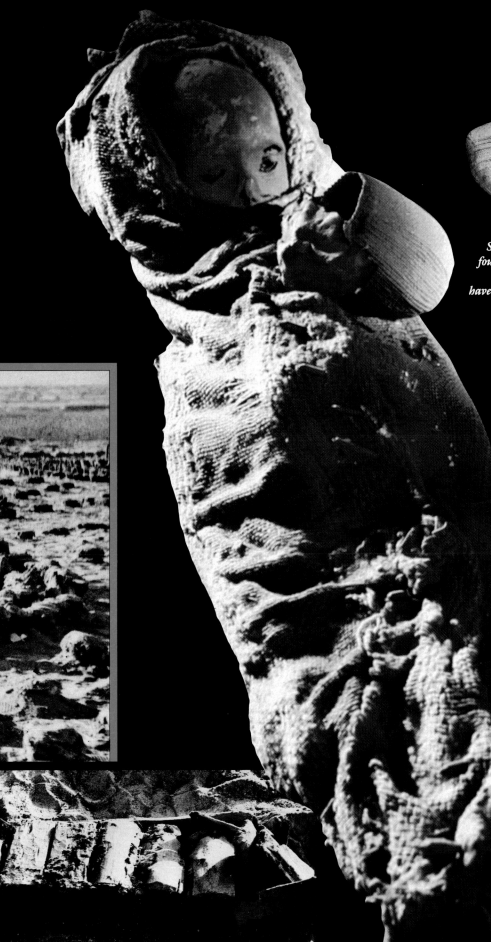

Wrapped in a woolen blanket held fast with 16 wooden pins, the mummy of a four- or five-year-old lies in repose just as it did for more than 4,000 years in the grave seen below at left. A basket containing grain accompanied the child in death.

The 3,800-year-old mummy of the woman below, dubbed the Eternal Beauty of Lou-lan for her striking Caucasian features, wore clothing and shoes of sheepskin and a woolen hat decorated with goose feathers when she was exhumed from one of the city's graves (right). An autopsy on the four-foot-nine-inch-tall, 40- to 45-year-old woman revealed desert dust and soot in her lungs and nits in her hair but could not pinpoint the cause of death.

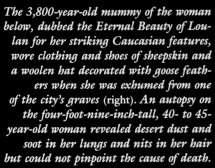

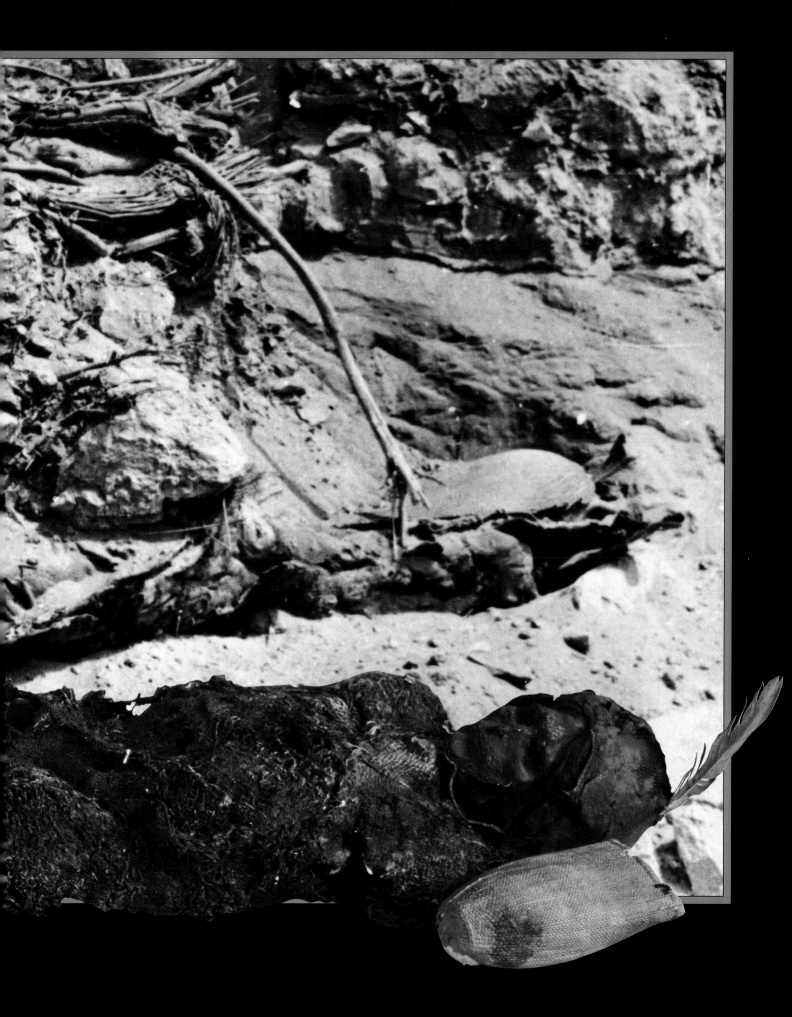

However out of the way they may seem today, the Taklamakan and Lop deserts were cultural crossroads, meeting points between East and West where ideas and goods were exchanged. But for all their vitality, they were turned by nature into a virtual no man's land, a sinister place to avoid at all costs. An Indian government report filed in 1875 recounts the tale of a shepherd who claimed to have beheld a lost city in the salt marshes of Lop Nor, remnants of an ancient lake. The shepherd did not enter the city, fearful death would befall him as supposedly it had others who dared do so. Even Marco Polo, who passed near the already sand-covered city of Loulan in the late 13th century AD, referred to the surrounding desert as ghoul-infested.

Superstition did not hold back Sven Hedin and Aurel Stein. They and those who followed eventually carted off tons of antiquities to museums around the world. For that reason, by the 1930s the Chinese banned any foreign explorations or excavations in the area, and it was not until 1979 that large-scale archaeological activity resumed. Recent joint expeditions of Chinese and Japanese scholars have made astonishing discoveries that point to widespread trade and communication at sites around the Taklamakan—places such as Kongque, Niya, and Qiemo, all once-verdant oases on the Silk Road.

Carrying their supplies on their backs, a joint expedition of Chinese and Japanese archaeologists traverse the lunarlike terrain of the Lop Desert. The team included one of the first groups of foreigners permitted by the Chinese government to dig in the area.

A 2,800-year-old rack of uncooked mutton on a 19-inch wooden skewer from a Qiemo tomb illustrates the ninth-century BC practice of providing sustenance for the dead and a grilling method of the day.

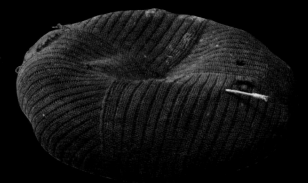

A black woven-wool cap from Qiemo, divided into four sections, sports a stalk of grass stuck into it like a hatpin. The oldest woven hat in China, it has a rim that still retains some elasticity.

Although yellowed with age, a sweaterlike woven-wool coat from ninth-century BC Qiemo still holds together. The garment is composed of five separate pieces of fabric.

A cowhide shoe, one of many remarkable objects uncovered in 1986 at Qiemo, shows signs of having been well made, with beautifully crafted sole and side seams.

A practical yet artfully decorated wooden spindle still holds on its shaft the leftover red wool spun ages ago by the skilled hand of a Qiemo weaver.

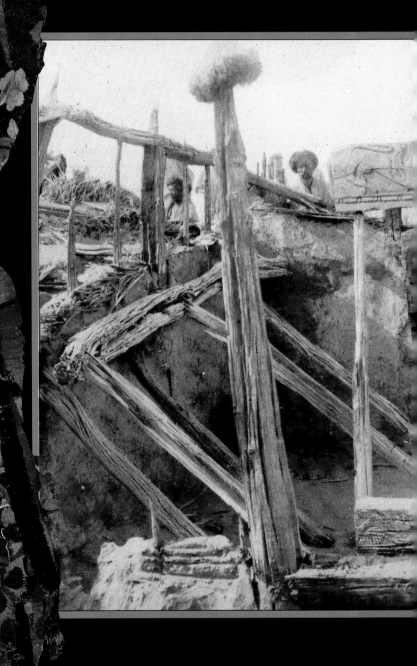

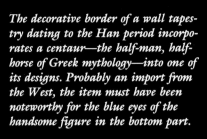

The decorative border of a wall tapestry dating to the Han period incorporates a centaur—the half-man, half-horse of Greek mythology—into one of its designs. Probably an import from the West, the item must have been noteworthy for the blue eyes of the handsome figure in the bottom part.

The colorful motifs as well as the weaving methods used to make this Han-era woolen saddlecloth indicate a strong Turkish influence. The 2,000-year-old cloth, made to be used over a saddle or in place of one, is amazingly well preserved.

Carved decorative elements and turned columns in wooden houses excavated at Niya by Aurel Stein display Greek, Persian, and Indian designs. The 1906 photo includes a beam bearing a relief of mythical beasts that Stein described in Eurocentric fashion as "Indo-Corinthian."

Indian script covers the surface of a Han-period letter written on wood (below, bottom). For security, two pieces of a wooden envelope were fitted over the tablet, tied round with rope, and held with clay impressed with the seal of the sender (below, top). The content of this document from Niya regards a tax matter and bears the seal of Lyipeya, Collector of Taxes.

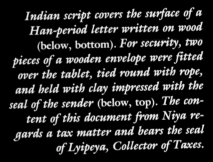

THE QIN: ONE TIME IN TEN THOUSAND GENERATIONS

Dating from the third century BC, this stable boy is one of thousands of terra-cotta figures buried around the tomb of Qin Shihuangdi, the first emperor of China. Archaeologists unearthed the figure in a six-foot-deep trench in 1976.

Digging a well about a mile east of the 150-foot-tall tumulus that marks the burial place of China's first emperor, Qin Shihuangdi, east of the city of Xi'an in China's northern Shaanxi Province, a farmer and his 10-year-old son struck something large and hard. Muddy water at the bottom of the shaft initially prevented them from making out what the object was. But as they tunneled past it, a clay shape emerged—that of a life-size man dressed in ancient military garb. Excited by their discovery, the pair continued burrowing until, suddenly and mysteriously, the water in the pit drained away. At this, the father decided that the half-buried statue was a demon of some sort and that it had to be punished, so he dug out the figure completely and exposed it to the blazing sun—and an unrecorded fate.

Sixty years would pass before members of a commune sinking another well, in March 1974, made a similar discovery in the same area. They had gone down approximately 13 feet when their tools clanked unexpectedly against chunks of terra cotta that to their astonishment proved to be fragments of broken life-size statues of uniformed soldiers and their horses.

The well diggers stopped work immediately and reported their find to local authorities, who summoned government archaeologists. The experts enlarged the trench and fanned out across the area to dig test holes, with stunning results. The site the peasants discovered, it was announced, occupied but a fraction of an immense, rectangular pit extending more than 200 feet from north to south and 760 feet from east to west.

Preliminary excavation revealed that 10 broad, rammed-earth walls ran the length of an underground chamber whose soil-covered roof had collapsed long ago as a result of fire. The walls divided the trench into 11 corridors. Each corridor contained dozens, if not hundreds, of pottery figures, along with bronze three-faced crossbow arrow tips, T-shaped halberd heads, swords, and other weapons, many still bright, sharp, and hard after centuries in the ground. The clay horses were positioned four abreast in six of the corridors; immediately behind them the archaeologists discovered remnants of two-wheeled wooden chariots.

The excitement attending the investigators' work heightened with the discovery of two additional trenches in May and June of 1976. Test excavations revealed that the first of these, located 65 feet north of the original chamber's eastern end, sheltered file after file of horse-drawn battle wagons, cavalry, and formations of kneeling archers and striding infantrymen. The small, U-shaped third pit lay almost 400 feet west of the second. It housed only one chariot and 64 terra-cotta soldiers but held a tantalizing mix of 30 prism-pointed spearheads, deer antlers, animal bones, and bronze rings from which curtains may once have been hung. A fourth pit, positioned between the second and third, proved incompletely dug and empty, as though work on it had been interrupted.

The find's magnitude promised to rival that of the First Emperor's burial mound itself, which, though unexcavated, was described in detail in *Shiji*, or *Records of the Historian*, an account written about a century after his death in 210 BC. "More than 700,000 con-

Qin Shihuangdi (below in an imaginary woodblock portrait made in AD 1609) ascended to the throne of Qin in 246 BC, when he was 13. His father's armies had already occupied the neighboring states Shu and Ba and annexed the territory of the Zhou, setting a pattern of subjugation the young ruler would extend to all the so-called Warring States in his effort to bring them under one rule.

scripts from all parts of the country worked there," the text relates. "The tomb was filled with models of palaces, pavilions, and offices, as well as fine vessels, precious stones, and rarities. Artisans were ordered to fix up crossbows so that any thief breaking in would be shot. All the country's streams, including the Yellow River and the Yangzi, were reproduced in quicksilver and by some mechanical means made to flow into a miniature ocean. The heavenly constellations were shown above and the regions of the earth below."

Although it was common at the time for surrogates of a king's courtiers and attendants to be buried with him so that they might continue to do his bidding in the afterworld, the account makes no mention of clay soldiers or horses. But it did offer archaeologists a clue: When the emperor learned that workers had nearly finished his tomb, the text says, he ordered them to lay the boundary of the surrounding funerary precinct 3,000 feet farther from the mausoleum complex. Therefore, the newly discovered pits were parts of the emperor's necropolis, and the terra-cotta multitude they harbored likely represented a guard from his vaunted fighting force.

Here at last was physical evidence that could be checked against ancient texts in a search for the truth. Since most of these were written either by Qin Shihuangdi's adversaries or long after the events recounted, the texts could be expected to contain embellishments of the facts, distortions of history, and lies. Now scholars could gaze upon an exacting reproduction of the army that made the First Emperor one of China's most celebrated and reviled rulers. Before their eyes, stretched row upon row, were the archers, horsemen, foot soldiers, and charioteers who shattered a congeries of independent kingdoms between 230 and 221 BC, initiating an astonishingly rapid—and enduring—transformation of Chinese society. In their numbers the silent figures demonstrated the unprecedented wealth and power enjoyed by the First Emperor, while he, his advisers, and his successors played out a drama of intrigue, obsession, greed, and betrayal, one that opened in epoch-making triumph, then abruptly closed after only 15 years. In the 2,000 years that dynasties controlled all or parts of China, few reigns were shorter lived, more tumultuous, or more influential.

Writing in 266 BC, seven years before Qin Shihuangdi was born, a nobleman in the state of Wei, Qin's rival to the immediate east, complained that Qin "has the heart of a tiger or a wolf.

It is avaricious, perverse, eager for profit, and without sincerity. It knows nothing about etiquette, proper relationships, and virtuous conduct, and if there be an opportunity for material gain, it will disregard its relatives as if they were animals." Whatever the veracity of the Wei nobleman's statement, Qin was certainly different. Ever since the city of Xianyang had become the Qin capital almost a hundred years earlier, a portion of the land had been administered not by hereditary lords, as had been traditional, but by 31 magistrates who were appointed—and controlled—by a centralized authority. New codified laws, posted on special pillars erected in Xianyang, replaced customary, largely unwritten, rules of behavior, and harsh discipline—such as flogging, mutilation, forced labor, castration, decapitation, and other torments—was to be meted out to all offenders, regardless of family prerogative or social status. "The punishments," an ancient text relates, "did not spare the strong and great."

This impersonal, impartial notion of government, later called Legalism, arose from the theory advocated by Shang Yang, the former government official from Wei who upon settling in Qin had become its chancellor in 359 BC. As trusted adviser to Duke Xiao, then ruler of Qin, Shang Yang instituted radical reforms that paved the way for the land's transition from an outpost on the western periphery of the central states to the hub of an empire. One of the most important was the abolition of the fixed landholding system, a measure that further diminished the power of the lords and lured rich peasants from other kingdoms to Qin because it made legal, for the first time, the buying and selling of farmland.

Gradually, old noble families declined, and persons of more humble origin came to the fore. The most famous of these was an ambitious official by the name of Li Si. While working as a government clerk in his native state of Chu, in south-central China, he observed that the rats living in the latrine near his quarters were easily

A passageway dug by modern farmers bisects the rammed-earth wall that the First Emperor ordered built to repel invaders from the north and to mark the border of his unified empire. Ancient texts say the bulwark stretched 2,600 miles—from Lintao, a city to the west of Xianyang, the capital, to the Liaodong Peninsula at the northern end of the Yellow Sea—but scholars now regard this as an exaggeration.

Iron collars such as this one, unearthed in 1973 near the First Emperor's burial complex, marked as convicts the laborers who worked on his funeral monument, great wall, and other construction projects. Designed to be an affliction, the ring weighs almost a pound, and its opening is less than four inches wide.

frightened whenever anyone approached, but the vermin that infested the granaries were bold and confident, fearing neither people nor dogs. "A man's ability or nonability," he concluded, "is similar to the condition of these rats. It merely depends upon where he places himself."

Taking this to heart, Li Si sought out Xun Qing, reputed to be one of the greatest scholars of the age, in order to learn how governments worked and to pick a kingdom where he, like the rats that feasted on grain, might prosper. The obvious choice, according to the wise man, was the kingdom of Qin. "Its frontier defenses," Xun Qing said, "are precipitous, its geographical configurations are advantageous, its mountains, forests, streams, and valleys are excellent, and its natural resources are abundant." In addition, Qin's people "stand in deep awe of their officials," whom the scholar found to be "courteous, temperate, honest, serious, sincere, and tolerant."

No doubt, Li Si was also aware that centuries of grim warfare with the pastoral peoples who resided north and west of Qin had had a profound effect on the development of its army and the honing of its tactics. Because these tribes fought on horseback in country that frequently was too rugged and hilly for chariots, the Qin learned to use mounted archers to combat the nomads. In addition, the tribes had no use for the rules of chivalry that were observed by the aristocrats who traditionally led China's feudal armies, so the Qin put professional generals in command of their troops and promoted men not on the basis of heredity or feudal standing but by the number of enemy heads they severed in combat. "Thus it is no accident, but calculation, that has made Qin victorious during four generations," Xun Qing counseled. "The apogee of good government is one in which there is repose and yet government; a general grasp of the situation and yet a going into details; an obtaining of results and yet an avoidance of bother. Qin is like this."

Li Si resolved to travel to Qin. Its king, he realized, "desires to swallow the world and to rule with the title of emperor. This is the time for commoners to be busy. It is the golden age of traveling politicians." He arrived in 247 BC, just at the death of King Zhuangxiang, and succeeded in attaching himself to Lü Buwei, the powerful chief counselor to 13-year-old Crown Prince Zheng, who succeeded his father to the throne. Li Si, in his first speech, urged the monarch to pursue his dreams of forging an empire. "With Qin's might and its great king's ability," he said, "the conquest of the other states would be like sweeping the dust from the top of a kitchen stove. Qin's power is sufficient to obliterate the feudal lords, bring to reality the imperial heritage, and make the world a single unity. This is the one time in 10,000 generations."

Li Si steadily gained the favor of the young king over the following years but remained in the shadow of Lü Buwei until 238 BC, when Zheng finally reached the age of maturity. That year, the chancellor was implicated in a sex scandal involving the king's widowed mother and a rebellious marquis named Lao Ai. Lü Buwei was forced into exile and later committed suicide by drinking poison.

Named minister of justice, Li Si continued to push the notion of unification, and King Zheng proved an adept listener. He adopted Li Si's bold vision and in the 17 years that lay ahead made it work. "As a silkworm devours a mulberry leaf," relates *Records of the Historian,* the young king's forces vanquished the six other great states. Han fell first, in 230 BC, followed by Zhao in 228, Wei in 225, and Chu in 223. The state of Yan, in the far northeast, collapsed next, in 222 BC. Then in 221 BC the armies of Qin conquered Qi, the last remaining kingdom. Some historians believe that untold hundreds of thousands lost their lives or were taken prisoner during these struggles, which extended King Zheng's domain from the western tablelands to the eastern ocean, an expanse of some 1,200 miles, and made him the first ever to rule a united China.

"Insignificant as I am," Zheng proclaimed with false modesty, "I have raised troops to punish the rebellious princes, and with the aid of the sacred power of our ancestors have punished them as they deserved, so that at last the empire is pacified." Such a conquest, he believed, had no parallel in history and merited a new name for himself. How else, the king asked his advisers, could his achievements be preserved for posterity?

Based on his counselors' advice, Zheng took the title *huang,* or august sovereign, to show his ascendancy over a mere *wang,* or king, and he augmented it with *shi,* meaning first, and *di,* which over a millennium had evolved to mean emperor after earlier signifying divine ruler or high god. In doing so, he gathered to himself the immense prestige of one of the giants of ancient Chinese myth and traditional history—Huangdi, the Yellow Emperor. According to

The palace seen above in an architect's restoration, located on a bluff overlooking the river Wei in Xianyang, served as one of the First Emperor's many abodes. But judging from signs of repeated repairs and renovations, archaeologists believe that the building in fact predated him and was erected by a Qin king who reigned in the Warring States period.

A clay tile with a molded grid of circles and double spirals lies at the foot of a step that once led from a covered walkway to rooms on the first level of the palace pictured at the top of the opposite page. Walls are visible in the background; on some, archaeologists found fragments of murals considered to be among the oldest in China.

legend, long before the Zhou, Shang, and Xia dynasties, Huangdi presided over an unprecedented age of achievement, during which ideal government institutions were established, writing was invented, and the first coins were minted. Then, after bringing order to earth, he is said to have risen into the sky as a *xian,* or immortal.

Huangdi's grand fate, the newly named Qin Shihuangdi believed, awaited him and his descendants. "We are the First Emperor," he announced grandly, "and our successors shall be known as the Second Emperor, Third Emperor, and so on, for endless generations." Like Huangdi, he and his followers would shape a new Chinese world—and not surprisingly, it would be one that closely resembled the state of Qin.

After unification, Qin Shihuangdi moved swiftly to eliminate the feudal lords with whom he had previously competed. Guided by Li Si, who was promoted from minister of justice to grand counselor, the First Emperor, in 221 BC, divided his realm into 36 commanderies and appointed a civil governor, a military commander, and an imperial inspector to administer each one. The policy—known as "strengthening the trunk and weakening the branches"—dramatically increased the power of the center and stripped members of the local aristocracy of their hereditary authority.

According to *Records of the Historian,* "The powerful and rich people of the empire, amounting to 120,000 families," were forced to quit their ancestral seats and move to Xianyang, now the imperial capital, where an eye could be kept on them and palaces were specially constructed for their use. After each feudal state was smashed, the ancient text reports, Qin Shihuangdi ordered a replica of the defeated ruler's palace erected on the bluffs overlooking the Wei River in Xianyang—a claim modern archaeology seems to support. Investigations conducted near the city have turned up 27 broad rammed-earth foundations, any number of which could have supported such a palace, and brought to light floor tiles that bear symbols of at least two of the vanquished kingdoms, Chu and Li Si's own Wei.

At the same time, the emperor ordered the defensive walls of cities and those separating the former kingdoms demolished and all civilian weapons confiscated. Legend has it that the arms were transported to Xianyang, melted down, and then cast into 12 enormous human statues that weighed more than 32 tons each. Colossal in size, rich in symbolism, the figures supposedly stood on the grounds of one of the imperial palaces, but archaeologists have yet to find evidence that the statues existed.

No such doubt exists regarding Qin Shihuangdi's sweeping social reforms, enacted in 221 BC as well, which were aimed at wiping out the prominent regional differences that divided his empire. If China were to be one country, ruled by a single system of laws and standards, then Qin's notion of universal, standardized law would have to apply to all of it. Consequently, the emperor imposed a single currency—a small bronze disk pierced with a square hole—throughout China *(pages 92-93)*.

In addition, Qin Shihuangdi established the script customary in Qin as the official writing system, doing away with regional variations and reducing the number of characters in use across China by about 25 percent *(pages 63-65)*. Some historians believe this reform, which was preserved by subsequent dynasties, was the most decisive of all because it prevented the variants from developing into separate forms of writing, an occurrence that would have doomed any possibility of long-term unity in a country as big as China.

On the strength of excavations conducted over the centuries, scholars also credit Qin Shihuangdi with standardizing the empire's system of weights and measures. The digs have unearthed bronze and terra-cotta measuring cups used to portion out grains and liquids, as well as bronze and iron weights employed to balance scales. Many carry the text of an imperial edict. "In the 26th year" of his reign, it reads, "the emperor completely unified the lords of the empire, the common people were at ease, and he was designated as huangdi, or sovereign emperor. And he issued an edict to his ministers: Standardize measurements. When they are not uniform or are in doubt, make them clear and uniform."

Most of the balance weights are metal bell shapes topped with loops and inscribed with the characters composing the decree. Smaller ones have special flanges to accommodate the text, and some lighter ones have sides large enough to fit the inscription but are hollow. The introduction of such weights no doubt extended the

reach of imperial law quite far into the people's lives, as did the enforcement of the First Emperor's many other reforms, but just how far remained unclear until December of 1975, when workers who were digging a drainage canal near the city of Yunmeng in central Hubei Province made a startling discovery.

The workers had chanced upon a group of graves, one of which, archaeologists said, contained the remains of a man who was laid to rest in 217 BC—four years after unifica-

tion. Alongside his chest and thighs, beside his head, under his belly, and elsewhere in the coffin lay 1,155 nine-inch-long bamboo slips. Stains at the top, middle, and bottom of the slivers indicated that three strings, long since deteriorated, originally bound the strips together so that they formed the pages of a book. Each slip contained as many as 40 characters, written in a single column in black, pine-soot ink, evidently with a rabbit-hair brush.

The texts suggest that the tomb's occupant was a lifelong Qin bu-

Located between foundations of layered, rammed earth at the west end of the First Emperor's burial complex, the drainage duct above is thought to have led water away from a building in which ceremonial food was prepared. The channel was composed of two-foot-long pottery segments such as this one placed end to end about three feet below ground.

reaucrat named Xi who took a job as a government scribe in 244 BC, rose to the rank of prefectural clerk three years later, and ultimately assumed the position of a subordinate official in one of the commanderies, a post he held from 235 BC until his death. Responsible for the management and control of government granaries and the distribution of grain stored there, Xi also tried criminal cases and oversaw the formation and feeding of labor crews. More than half of the bamboo slips he took to the afterworld, archaeologists believe, are the legal and administrative documents he consulted while attending to his earthly duties.

Although only a selection from a much larger body of laws, the bamboo texts provide telling glimpses of what life was like for Xi as an official of China's first empire. The ruling Legalists had insisted upon quantitative exactitude and administrative efficiency in the state of Qin; now they demanded the same throughout all of China. Royal commands and documents marked "urgent," for example, were to be forwarded without delay, a statute read, and all documents were to be marked with the month, day, and time of their sending and arrival "so as to expedite a reply."

Other regulations found in Xi's tomb revealed the government's intense interest in agriculture. Rules required local authorities to report regularly on the size of harvests, the health of livestock, and the death of horses, and spelled out stiff punishments for not safeguarding nature's bounty. "When a granary leaks," one ordinance specifies, "causing rot among the grain, as well as when piling up grain one lets it become spoilt, then in case the inedible part is less than 100 bushels, the overseer of the office is reprimanded." If the amount lost totaled more than 100 bushels, however, a fine was levied, payable not with cash coins but with a suit of armor.

As documents from other sources show, even harsher retribution awaited those who broke the law of weights and measures. Many were sent off to work on the palaces the emperor ordered erected in and around Xianyang or to toil on even more ambitious construction projects, such as the empire's new road system, which was designed to facilitate communication with distant outposts. Beginning in 220 BC thousands of convict and corvée laborers extended spokelike thoroughfares of rammed earth from Xianyang in the west to the north, northeast, east, and southeast. When finished, the roads measured 38 feet across and covered almost 5,000 miles.

Remnants of the main 500-mile northbound highway, called

SURPRISING SHAPES FOR MONEY

Long before they had coins, the Chinese used grain, cloth, and cowrie shells, among other valuable commodities, in exchange for goods and labor. Indeed, wages were often paid in grain. But by the fourth century BC, commerce had grown so much that all of the great states began issuing coins of their own, often with holes in them so the pieces could be conveniently strung together and suspended from belts. Such coins had wide circulation as revealed by a hoard, discovered in the 1960s in a jar, that consisted of the currencies of almost all the states of the day.

Generally cast in bronze, these early coins exhibited a variety of unusual shapes, some replicating objects from daily life. The *wuan* above, minted in the state of Zhao, was designed to look like a spade. The coin from the state of Chu (*upper right*) mimics a spade as well, but the seven-inch-long

bronze *dao (below)*, circulated in three adjacent states, has a knife-like form stamped with the words "legally approved at Anyang." There was even a coin, known as "the ant's nose," produced in the shape of a cowrie shell.

After the First Emperor united the states that had been contending with one another for years, he imposed a unified currency that facilitated the development of a national economy and encouraged widespread trading. The shape of one piece, the round *banliang* above, proved so practical that it became the standard for Chinese coins—and has remained so right up to modern times.

the Straight Road, are still in existence today. According to *Records of the Historian*, the road's surface was salted with the sweat of no fewer than 300,000 convict laborers. Slaving under the grueling command of General Meng Tian, leader of the Qin forces that had overrun Qi in 221 BC, they were allowed to put aside their road-building tools for two reasons only—to take up arms against the Rong and other so-called barbarians, and to work on the Long Wall *(page 86),* the general's third great project. Constructed by consolidating perimeter walls built over the years by the rulers of Wei, Zhao, Yan, and other states, the fortification ultimately stretched along most of China's northern border.

Ancient texts say only one other Qin-era work force rivaled Meng Tian's army in terms of size: the 700,000 convicts and sundry laborers who built Qin Shihuangdi's colossal mausoleum. They first started construction in 246 BC, when as a boy Zheng inherited the Qin throne, yet still had not completed the complex when the emperor died 36 years later. Archaeologists can only speculate about what the laborers might have accomplished had they been allowed more time, yet no one disputes that they did in fact create one of the world's great wonders—the terra-cotta army.

Ever since the site was officially discovered in 1974, archaeologists have been busy unearthing, documenting, and painstakingly preserving the figures. The work is still far from complete—and in some respects, it is hardly begun. Yet scholars have already taken from it valuable insights into the composition of Qin Shihuangdi's army and into its weapons and tactics.

Pit 1, the rectangular vault initially penetrated by the archaeologists, has been studied the most. It contains the main fighting force of the underground army—estimated to be at least 6,000 pottery figures in all, more than 200 of which form the unit's vanguard. Dressed in simple battle tunics, light shoes and leggings, and no armor, these troops stand shoulder to shoulder in three rows located at the pit's eastern end.

From the modeling of the bowmen's hands and the wealth of bronze crossbow triggers and arrow tips unearthed nearby, the scientists determined that each one originally held a crossbow—a 4½-foot-long wooden bow that was wrapped with leather strips and lacquered, then affixed to a slotted wooden stock. The weapon had a range of over half a mile, written sources say,

and generated 800 pounds of tension—more than enough to impale enemy armor. Indeed, some historians argue that the technology was first introduced to the West after arrows fired from similar crossbows easily pierced the shields used by Roman soldiers at the battle of Sogdiana, in central Asia, in 36 BC. On attack, the bowmen probably kept their distance, much like the users of modern long-range artillery, and doused the First Emperor's foes with a rain of lethal arrows.

Immediately behind this vanguard, 11 corridors extend to the west, six of which sheltered wooden horse-drawn chariots and an advance squad of foot soldiers. A pair of seven-pound bronze bells and the remnants of drums were found near two of the wagons, leading archaeologists to conclude that the carts were as much command vehicles as battle wagons—a proposition supported by historical sources. One drumbeat, for example, signaled the troops to start marching, texts say, while a second meant to commence the attack. Conversely, when a bell resonated, the soldiers were to cease fighting, and if it sounded again, they were to retreat.

Lightly armored infantrymen equipped with swords, lances, and axes make up the body of the terra-cotta formation. The very picture of strength achieved through numbers, they stand in rows of four behind the chariots and, in three corridors, behind squads of unarmored spearmen. Although today the statues appear a monotonous buff-gray, patches of paint still clinging here and there to the clay indicate that their outfits once gleamed with bright colors *(page 113)*—brown armor held by red ties, green or purple tunics and leggings, and brown or white hats tied with red or purple straps.

Protected from the elements by a huge, permanent structure, visitors in 1979 stand atop walkways built to provide access to Pit 1, while archaeologists work on terra-cotta figures in the corridors below. The railing in the foreground is part of an observation platform for tourists.

Two long files of battle-ready bowmen were discovered in the aisles at the pit's northern and southern ends, and test excavations suggest three rows of marksmen—a mirror image of the vanguard—were positioned in the west. On all sides, the archers along the edges face outward, rendering the inner mass of soldiers and horses virtually invulnerable to surprise from any direction. But this was not the formation's only advantage, military historians assert: It also enabled the Qin army to fight front against front, as well as to modify its configuration quickly and easily—into a V, for example, to envelop the enemy, or into an inverted V to punch through his center.

Preliminary probing and spot excavations have revealed that Pit 2, the vault lying immediately northeast of Pit 1, also contains a remarkable military assemblage. An estimated 80 archers, all of them resting on their right knee and gazing confidently eastward, are

By 1992 scientists had excavated about one third of Pit 1 and uncovered the artifacts schematically represented here: remnants of eight two-wheeled chariots and 32 horses, along with a host of armored (red) and unarmored (yellow) soldiers. With the exception of those positioned along the edges of the two parallel sides, every warrior faced east—toward the First Emperor's vanquished enemies.

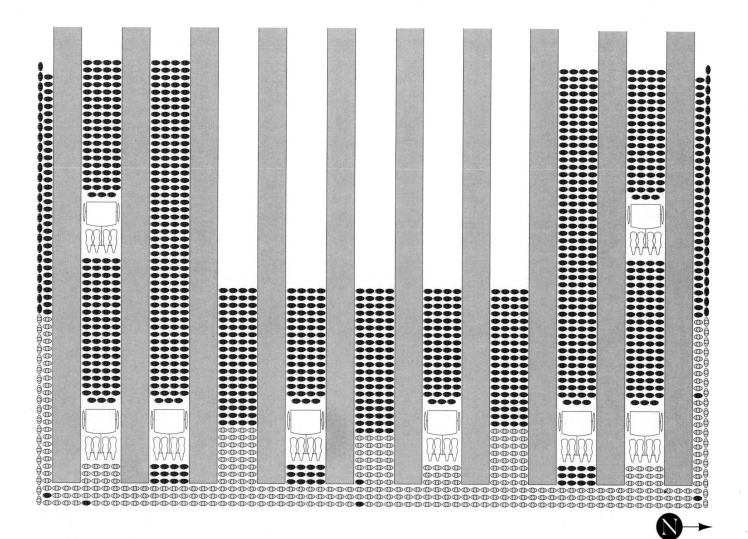

LIFELIKE SCULPTURE ON AN ASSEMBLY-LINE BASIS

Many of the pottery sherds—pieces of the First Emperor's terra-cotta army—that archaeologists have recovered from Pits 1, 2, and 3 have provided valuable clues as to how this extraordinary military force was created 22 centuries ago. For example, of the heads of horses and soldiers that fractured, almost all of them split cleanly into halves. Those of the horses broke along a seam running between the eyes and the nostrils, those of the men along a line that originates at either side of the neck, passes just behind the ears, and crosses at the top of the head. Fingerprints found inside many of the halves have led archaeologists to conclude that workers formed the heads by pressing damp clay into molds.

Body fragments have proved equally illuminating. Straw imprints on the interior of horses permit speculation that the animals may have been shaped on straw-covered forms. Rope marks winding around the thighs of some warriors suggest that rope may have been used to bolster the legs' load-bearing capability until the clay hardened in the kiln. Afterward, the imprints would have been concealed by the soldiers' tunics.

Four hundred seventy-nine inscriptions were inconspicuously stamped or scratched on different body parts. Of these, 230 are numbers that probably helped the emperor's recordkeepers monitor productivity. The remainder specify the names of 85 separate master artisans, each of whom, researchers assume, supervised a team of 10 to 12 assistants.

According to historical texts, the majority of these workers were not potters by trade but forced laborers or convicts. To accommodate their lack of skills and still meet a stiff production schedule, most workshops broke the creative process into a series of steps similar to those shown at right in modern recreations set up at the excavation-site museum. Only a few of the steps, archaeologists believe, required the technical know-how and deft touch of an artisan.

A cavalryman stands with his mount. When the pair was excavated in Pit 2 in 1977, the horse was still holding the bronze bridle bit in its mouth.

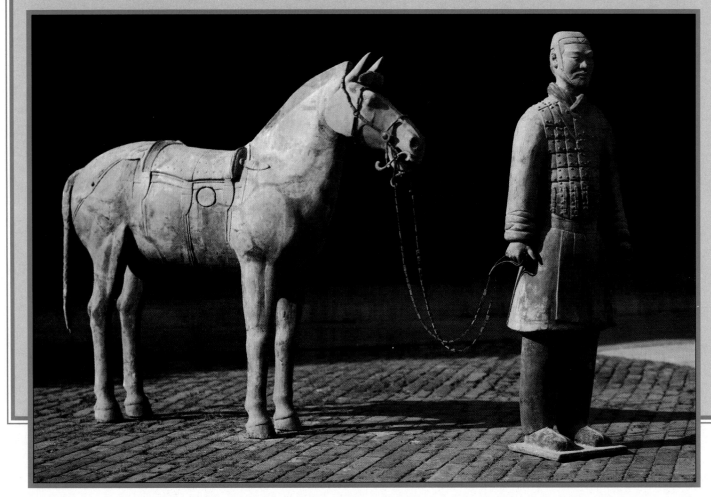

Hands on shoulders, five laborers start the creation process by stamping fresh clay with their feet to mix it and drive out air bubbles (1). Other workers pound the material into long sheets (2), which assistants lay over a rough straw-covered frame and begin molding into the shape of a horse's belly and hindquarters (3). A wooden scaffold bears the growing weight of the life-size sculpture.

Artisans remove straw from the interior and smooth the outside but leave a circular hole in the horse's flank (4), perhaps to facilitate the flow of hot gases during firing later. From molds, other laborers fashion a hollow neck and solid legs (5) and affix them to the torso using a thin layer of wet clay (6).

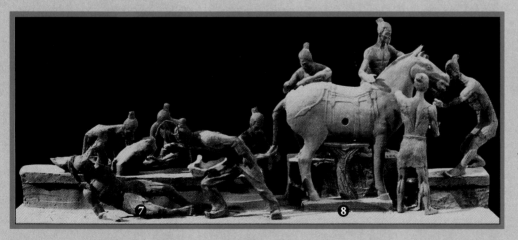

Two workers fasten a hand-modeled lower jaw to the head, which consists of half sections that had been formed in molds (7). Ears made from thin sheets of rolled clay are added. Then, after pressing a mold directly against the horse's back to create a saddle and supplying a forelock, the potters finish the job by setting the head in place and inserting a plaited tail (8).

situated in a square formation in the chamber's northeast corner, surrounded on all sides by striding, unarmored foot soldiers.

To the archers' west stands a mixed force of chariots, infantry, and cavalry—armored soldiers who at one time held a crossbow in their left hand and the reins of a terra-cotta horse in their right. Such troops, military historians assert, were key players during the Changping campaign, waged by the kingdoms of Qin and Zhao a year before the First Emperor was born. At the conflict's conclusion, a special detachment of 25,000 Qin charioteers and infantrymen pursued the retreating Zhao army, and 5,000 cavalrymen rode against the enemy's defensive encampments, with decisive and bloody results. The Zhao force was divided, its supply line severed.

The eight southernmost corridors of Pit 2 are thought to house only chariots and charioteers. Test excavations conducted to date have unearthed neither command instruments nor any of the foot soldiers who accompany similar vehicles in Pit 1. These results have led some scholars to assume that the chariots in Pit 2 were intended to represent a reserve force.

Originally, dozens of armed soldiers—their heels pressed to the walls and their eyes fixed forward—stood at attention in the southern wing of U-shaped Pit 3, the smallest of the three chambers containing figures. Two files of 11 warriors waited in a similar corridor to the north. And near the center of the vault, archaeologists have discovered the remnants of one covered chariot hitched to a team of four terra-cotta horses.

Military historians believe the Pit 3 soldiers are standing watch over the command center for the entire terra-cotta army and that such a chariot would probably have been used to rush orders to troops in the field. Yet the presence here of deer antlers and animal bones has led investigators to conclude that Pit 3 also had a second purpose, that of a special meeting place where sacrifices and prayers were offered and attempts were made to predict the outcome of upcoming battles. Historians have few doubts that such practices fascinated the First Emperor. Yet it appears unlikely that any rite of divination could have foretold the speed with which his reign—and his infant dynasty—would come to an end.

According to *Records of the Historian,* the trouble started at an imperial banquet in 213 BC, when one of the guests, a scholar from the former kingdom of Qi, a traditional center of Confucianism, openly

Discovered in the ground around the terra-cotta warriors, dozens of seven-inch-long bronze arrowheads await excavation. So far, archaeologists at work in Pits 1, 2, and 3 have unearthed more than 10,000 such tips, along with crossbow triggers, swords, spears, signaling bells, and other paraphernalia of war.

criticized the First Emperor. He pointed out that while the sons and brothers of Qin Shihuangdi remained commoners, the offspring, siblings, and ministers of the Shang and Zhou kings had been given fiefs and that these rewards had contributed to the stability and staying power of the early dynasties. "Nothing can endure for long," he concluded, "but that which is modeled on antiquity."

Outraged, the emperor's grand counselor, Li Si, rose to rebut the academician's remarks. First, he praised the sovereign's many accomplishments, then he attacked the scholars. "There are some men of letters," the counselor accused, "who do not model themselves upon the present, but study the past in order to criticize the present age. They confuse and excite the ordinary people. If such conditions are not prohibited, the imperial power will decline above and partisanship will form below."

To preserve order and prevent insurrection, Li Si said, all histories, collections of odes and poems, and volumes of speculative thought should be handed over to the governors of the commanderies and burned, and persons found in possession of such writings should be branded and sent to do hard labor. Even discussing the forbidden works, Li Si suggested, should be made a crime punishable by execution followed by public display of the corpse. Only Qin historical records, volumes on medicine, divination, and agriculture, and works held in the bureau of the academicians were to be spared. "As for persons who wish to study," Li Si said, "let them take the officials as their teachers."

Historians today can only guess at how many texts were actually fed to the flames. But some believe that the damage done to the emperor's standing, especially among intellectuals—a large body of professionals whose very livelihood was imperiled by the decree—far outweighed the destruction of the works themselves. Seeking revenge, these individuals later wrote the histories of the Qin era that are peppered with exaggerations and out-and-out fabrications, including the notion that the First Emperor ordered the execution of 460 scholars in 212 BC by having them buried alive.

That the story was regarded as fact for centuries stems in part from the great gulf that apparently came to separate

A messenger entrusted with delivering the First Emperor's orders carried half of this inlaid bronze tally as a sign of his credibility. Along its inside were pyramid-shaped bosses that fit perfectly into recesses on the tiger's other half, which was held by the field commander who was to execute the order.

Qin Shihuangdi from the people he ruled. As king of Qin, he had barely escaped assassination at the hands of a dagger-wielding agent of the kingdom of Yan who wanted to halt Qin's rapid accumulation of power, and as emperor he survived two more attacks—one by an assailant seeking to avenge the death of the first assassin and another by a man whose family had been dishonored. Though unsuccessful, the assaults left scars: The First Emperor grew distrustful and reclusive. Then, in his later years, he is supposed to have removed himself from the public eye altogether in order to pursue a seductive but elusive goal—attaining immortality.

If this is truly what happened, Qin Shihuangdi would have regarded the quest as a legitimate expression of ancient tradition. According to many thinkers of the time, each person possesses two souls: the *hun,* which provides intelligence, and the *po,* which animates the flesh. As long as the body remains sound, the pair have a place to reside. But when the body fails, the hun rises to the heavens, and the po returns to the earth. In order to escape death, therefore, the souls must be prevented from separating by extending the life of the body. And this, the emperor was told, could be accomplished only by means of magical elixirs.

Now *Records of the Historian* begins to elaborate on what may be a kernel of truth, possibly resorting to the apocryphal for the sake of delivering a good story. But it is a story worth retelling for what it has to say about Chinese belief of the day. The history relates that the ruler summoned a host of magicians to his court to come up with the elixirs and that he traveled widely throughout the empire in search of eight immortal beings who, he hoped, would share with

Holding a jade disk symbolic of his authority, the future First Emperor, shown at right in this rubbing of a second-century AD stone relief, escapes with his life in 227 BC after the first of three assassination attempts. At left, a courtier restrains the king's assailant, who raises his arms in frustration after hurling his dagger into the pillar at center.

Seated in this silk painting thought to date from the 17th century AD, the First Emperor decides the fate of a blue-robed scholar, while outside the gates books are destroyed. The scene is largely fanciful: Ancient texts say the events occurred in different years, not at the same time, and the execution of scholars may not have taken place at all.

him the secrets of deathlessness. "The First Emperor wandered about the shore of the Eastern Sea and offered sacrifices to the famous mountains and the great rivers and the Eight Spirits and searched for the immortals," the text claims. It goes on to say that Qin Shihuangdi even equipped a fleet of ships and sent 3,000 young men and women to sea in hopes of locating three islands said to be the immortals' dwelling places. Although the expedition was never heard from again, legend holds that it colonized Japan.

Advised by magicians that his chances of becoming a divine being would be harmed so long as his subjects knew where he was, Qin Shihuangdi finally decided to remove himself as much as possible from mortal sight. He ordered all of his palaces in the vicinity of Xianyang linked by covered, walled passageways so he could move between them unseen, and he made it a capital crime for anyone to divulge his whereabouts. Thus the supreme ruler of the Chinese world unwittingly placed himself in the power of the few insiders who were privy to his itinerary. Just how much this self-imposed regime of secrecy imperiled the dynasty became clear in 210 BC, when at some point during his fifth tour of the realm, the emperor suddenly fell ill and died, and the members of his entourage—Prince Huhai, one of the ruler's younger sons; Zhao Gao, a eunuch who had served as Huhai's tutor; and Li Si—plotted to conceal his passing.

Records of the Historian suggests that a nefarious plot now changed the course of Chinese history. Instead of notifying the legitimate heir, Prince Fusu, who had been sent north to oversee the work of General Meng Tian, Zhao Gao and Li Si acted as though nothing had happened. They continued to enter the imperial litter, as if to consult with their sovereign and deliver food, and they issued an imperial edict naming the dim, manipulatable Huhai crown

prince. In a letter, they accused Fusu of being "unfilial" and Meng Tian of "lacking in rectitude" and demanded that the two commit suicide. Suspecting skulduggery, the general suggested that Fusu request confirmation, but the prince obediently carried out the order. "When a father allows his son to die," he asked before he took his life, "how can there be any question of sending back a request?"

By this time, the imperial litter was reeking terribly in the summer heat, reports *Records of the Historian;* to mask the stench, it is said, the plotters placed a wagon loaded with salted fish in the cortege. When Huhai finally reached the capital, he announced his father's death and proclaimed himself Erh Shihuangdi, the Second Sovereign Emperor. Then, as a special mark of honor and respect for the First Emperor, he ordered all his father's childless concubines and all the artisans who had labored to construct the mausoleum, and therefore knew of its rich treasures and secrets, buried with him.

Sadly for the Second Emperor, all order disappeared almost as soon as workers sealed the tomb's great door. In the late summer of 209 BC, a series of revolts erupted in the one-time kingdom of Chu, and unrest spread across the empire. The turmoil reached as far as the capital, where the scheming Zhao Gao and Li Si became embroiled in a bitter power struggle. In time, the eunuch persuaded the ruler to have Li Si thrown in prison. Beaten mercilessly, the statesman confessed to charges of planning a revolt and was sentenced to torture and a gruesome, public death. In 208 BC he was cut in two at the waist in the marketplace of Xianyang, and his parents, brothers, wife, and children were executed.

That year, a rebel army besieged a town only 30 miles from Xianyang. Members of a convict army still

Archaeologists document and preserve two bronze chariots and horses that were found in 1980, complete with drivers, in a 22-foot-long chamber on the west side of the First Emperor's tomb. Though only half-size, each chariot and team measured almost 11 feet long and weighed 2,700 pounds. A painted cloud pattern adorned the interior of the canopied chariot at top left, which stands below in reconstructed splendor.

laboring at the First Emperor's burial mound crushed the revolt but were powerless to chase away the cloud of intrigue that soon enveloped the imperial court. In 207 BC Zhao Gao made a grab for power by having fake bandits stage an attack on the palace to which the monarch had retired. In the ensuing confusion, the Second Emperor committed suicide. He was succeeded by his nephew Ziying, who took the title of king since he could not claim to rule a united empire.

By the end of the year, the ruler's ministers and princes deserted to the rebels, and the capital was again threatened, this time by forces under the command of a commoner named Liu Bang. Opting not to risk destruction of the city, Ziying bound his neck with a silken cord as a symbol of his readiness to hang himself and, accompanied by his wife and sons, surrendered peacefully. But then a second, much larger army under the command of Liu Bang's superior, Xiang Yu, came on the scene. Determined to end the Qin dynasty once and for all, Xiang Yu beheaded Ziying, and his troops sacked the capital, set fire to the palaces, and broke open the tomb of the First Emperor.

"After 30 days of plundering," an ancient history tells of the insurgents, "they still could not exhaust the contents of the mausoleum. Bandits melted the coffins for bronze as well as setting fire to it. The fire burned for more than 90 days." Archaeologists believe the blaze set in the pits containing the terra-cotta army so weakened the beams supporting the heavy, earthen roof that it collapsed, shattering many of the figures and burying them in rubble. The sherds would lie hidden until the well diggers of the local commune started work in 1974—almost 22 centuries later.

Outraged by such wanton acts of destruction, Liu Bang warred grimly for four years against Xiang Yu. Then, finally victorious, Liu Bang laid his claim to the title vacated by the Second Emperor, that of sole ruler of a unified empire. In doing so, he would establish one of the longest and most glorious periods in the country's history—the Han dynasty.

THE BURIED ARMY

One of the greatest archaeological finds of all time, the terra-cotta army of China's first emperor also has involved one of the biggest excavations ever carried out in that country. The site where the soldiers turned up encompasses 5½ square acres—and much of it yet remains to be excavated. Pit 1, where most of the digging has occurred, is some 16 feet deep, almost 760 feet long, and more than 200 feet wide. To create it and the other two pits in which figures have been found, the emperor's laborers removed more than 3½ million cubic feet of earth—enough to fill more than 36 Olympic swimming pools.

After excavating the pits, the workers threw soil back into the cavities and pounded it into 2-foot-thick, cement-hard floors and 10-foot-high perimeter walls. Some walls measure 8 feet through and still bear the imprint of the frames that held the soil as it was compacted. The workers also built broad interior walls partitioning Pits 1 and 2 into long, east-west-running corridors. Once the dividers were completed, masons covered the floor with some 250,000 rectangular bricks, taking pains to ensure those laid at the center of each aisle were higher than those along the sides so moisture would flow away from the standing figures.

To shelter the army, carpenters placed heavy pine or cedar posts into foot-deep holes dug at the base of the perimeter and partitioning walls and topped the vertical timbers with horizontal ones, forming joists. Crosswise over these, 40-foot-long beams were laid, then covered with woven bamboo or straw mats and an 11-inch layer of clay that now appears red—a probable effect of the fire that engulfed the site 2,200 years ago.

Wheel ruts on ramps leading to ground level hint that figures such as the warrior and horse above were rolled into place after the roof was sealed. Later, the inclines were blocked with posts, mats, and rammed earth, and the entire vault was buried—for eternity, or so the builders believed—under almost 10 feet of earth.

In 1975 archaeologists inspect pieces of soldiers unearthed in the east gallery of Pit 1 (left), while other workers take measurements atop the east-west-running partitioning walls.

Archaeologists gently brace the chin of a standing unarmored warrior, thought to be a spearman or a bowman, as they clean his head with brush and trowel.

Four fractured horses lie amid a jumble
of shattered and upright clay figures
in Pit 1. The equine team was originally
harnessed to a wooden chariot.

Freed from the soil, about 1,100 warriors and 32 horses stand in the eastern third of Pit 1. Experts estimate that at least 5,000 figures remain buried in the western part.

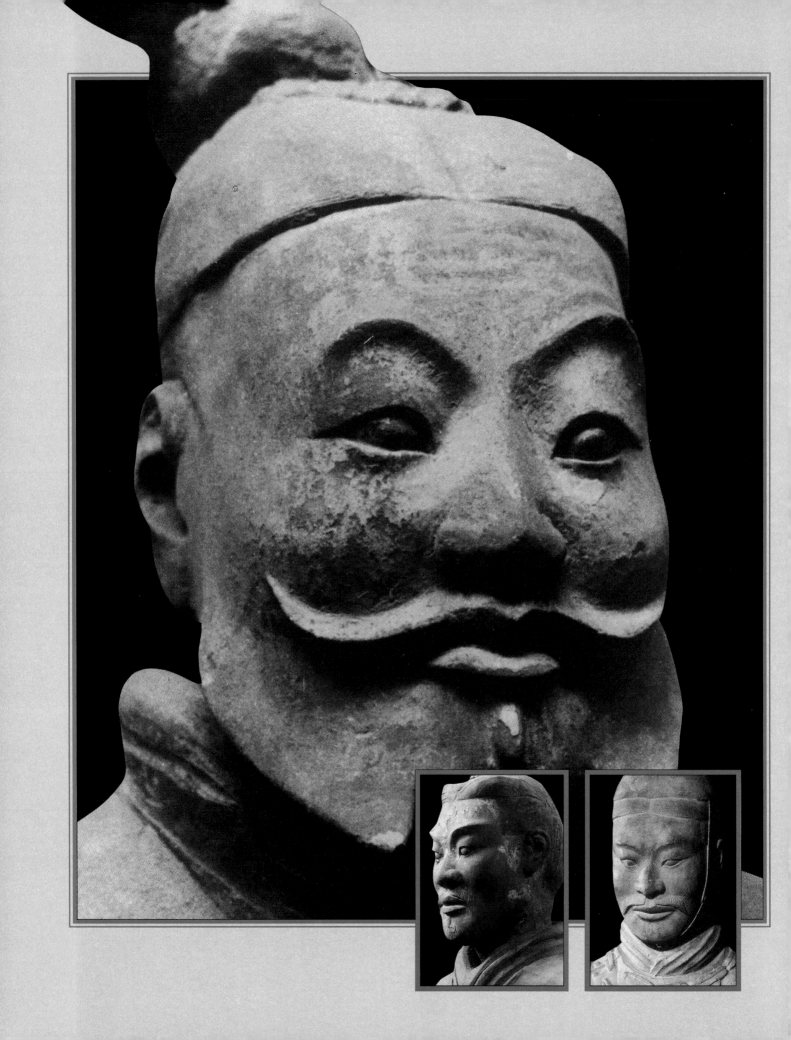

VARIED FACES OF FIGHTING MEN

Although every terra-cotta soldier is unique, many parts were mass produced. Each head, for example, consists of hollow front and rear sections fashioned from one of at least eight standardized molds. And the warriors' ears, noses, lips, eyebrows, and other features, including several types of beards and mustaches, were prefabricated as well. Potters made the features by hand and in molds and attached them to faces with a thin paste of clay and water. They also pressed molds directly into the unbaked heads to form hair and headdresses.

Scholars believe the sculptors were free to mix and match pieces as they wished and that certain heads were reshaped with knives and detailed with pointed tools. The resulting individuality of the subjects, as shown here and on the following pages, so astonished the archaeologists who first gazed upon the figures that a few wondered if soldiers had sat for portraits—perhaps in lieu of being buried alive.

The visages of these immortal warriors suggest the wide range of ages, homelands, and temperaments of the flesh-and-blood soldiers who made up the First Emperor's mighty army.

COMMANDER. *This officer once rested his hands on the hilt of a 35-inch-long bronze sword, remnants of which were unearthed nearby. His raised index finger is thought to have pointed at his troops. The headpiece, the tassels on his chest and shoulders, the intricate armor, and his size all speak for exalted rank; at six feet five inches, he is one of the tallest clay figures.*

CHARIOTEER. *Responsible for controlling the four-horse team that drew his battle chariot, this driver clutched two pairs of reins in each hand. The first pair ran between the thumb and index fingers; the second passed between his parted index and middle fingers. Like the commander, he wears a bonnet secured with an elaborate bow.*

ARCHER. *The softly folded fabric around the neck of this kneeling bowman, one of 24 unearthed in Pit 2 in 1977, kept his armor from chafing. Scholars cannot say if he cradled the bow in his left hand or if the weapon was slung around his chest and he held arrows. The added colors are based on traces of pigment discovered on the statue. All of the terra-cotta figures, horses included, were originally painted in vivid hues.*

INFANTRYMAN. *This unarmored warrior and dozens of figures like him were positioned in rows before a contingent of kneeling archers in Pit 2. Raising his arms and turning to the left, he seems to be practicing tai ji chuan, the martial art of shadowboxing. Yet bronze arrowheads and the remains of wooden longbows found in his vicinity leave little doubt that his mission was offensive.*

THE HAN: FLESH ON THE BONES OF HISTORY

Testifying to the Han gentry's growing wealth and social power, this 51-inch-high clay tower typifies building models that accompanied many rich landowners to their graves.

While members of a detachment of soldiers were climbing Mount Ling in May 1968, some 100 miles southwest of Beijing, they caught sight of something mysterious, an unnatural-looking crevice in the limestone, and paused for a closer examination. One soldier descended into the opening and found himself standing in a hand-hewn chamber. The authorities were notified, and teams of specialists from the province of Hebei's archaeology unit and from the Institute of Archaeology in Beijing arrived to investigate. Local civilians joined the experts and soldiers in removing two brick walls between which molten iron had been poured. Beyond was a tunnel boring into the heart of the mountain. At the far end of this dark and laboriously carved passageway, which was crammed with rock to further block entry, the party crossed an intersecting corridor containing the skeletons of 16 horses and the six two-wheeled carriages the animals had drawn. Directly ahead loomed an imposing central chamber. Measuring some 40 by 50 feet, it had once housed a wooden structure, now collapsed, that apparently had been erected to simulate part of a palace.

In a separate room behind the chamber the investigators made the most startling discovery of all. There lay the stone coffin of none other than Liu Sheng, a personage already known to Chinese historians as one of the sons of the emperor Jing, fourth monarch of the

Han dynasty, which ruled over China from 206 BC to AD 220 after the collapse of the Qin dynasty.

The emperor's son—who in 154 BC had become king of Zhongshan—had been laid to rest in a suit made of more than 2,000 jade plaques, which were threaded together with filaments of gold. The elaborate shroud had survived the centuries of interment, but Liu Sheng's body had completely disintegrated. Buried under the man-made cave's dust and rubble lay a trove of treasures—ceremonial knives and swords, traces of lustrous lacquerware, and handsome bronze vessels inlaid with golden dragons.

In a second richly appointed rock-cut tomb nearby, similarly blocked by a brick-and-iron door, the excavators discovered fragments of eight teeth, all that remained of Liu Sheng's consort, the princess Dou Wan. She too had been shrouded in a burial suit of jade and accompanied by stunning examples of Han artistry. There were wine vessels inlaid with gold and silver. A gilt-bronze phoenix, encrusted with green stones, clutched a jade ring in its beak. Most ingenious was a bronze lamp, in the shape of a kneeling servant girl, who held a cylindrical lantern that could be adjusted to change the direction and intensity of the light beam.

Researchers reckoned that the construction of the two burial chambers and the manufacture of the 2,800 items that the chambers contained would have required the concerted efforts of hundreds, if not thousands, of men and women. Each of the jade suits alone, according to the calculations of modern scholars, required some 10 years of labor to complete.

According to the Han dynasty's grand historian Sima Qian, "Liu Sheng loved to drink and was very fond of women." Liu Sheng himself did not see these traits as vices, and he lambasted his sibling the king of Zhao for taking far too great an interest in the dreary day-to-day business of government. "Although my brother is a king," admonished Liu Sheng, "he spends all his time doing the work of his own clerks and officials. A true king should pass his days listening to music and delighting himself with beautiful sights and sounds." The brother spurned this criticism. "The king of Zhongshan," he replied, "fritters away his days in sensual gratification, instead of assisting the Son of Heaven to bring order to the common people."

The argument reflects more than a mere brotherly squabble, as the archaeologist Robert L. Thorp has pointed out; it could serve as a metaphor for the achievements of the dynasty to which the pair

In the 1968 photo at right, archaeologists prepare to remove the brick wall, backed by iron, blocking the way into the 2,000-year-old tomb of Dou Wan, consort of Liu Sheng, son of a Han emperor. In the second picture, they are at work in Liu Sheng's tomb; the door in the background is the entrance to the burial chambers themselves. The third picture, taken inside the room containing Liu Sheng's coffin, shows his jade burial suit (detail below), still held together by gold wires.

belonged. For the 400-year-long era of the Han encompassed both polarities: It was an age when artists and artisans, the creators of Liu Sheng's "beautiful sights and sounds," flourished; equally, it was an epoch of practical accomplishments, marked by economic growth, intellectual achievement, explorations both geographical and philosophical, and technological advances.

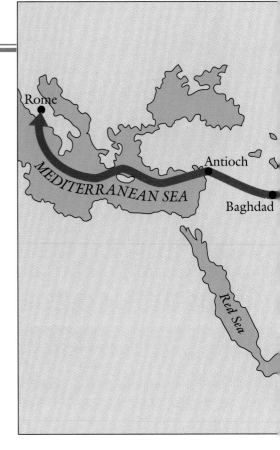

At its peak, the Han empire equaled in strength and glory the Roman Empire that flourished in the same era, far to the west. Earlier generations had forged the Chinese state and rendered it stable; the Han rulers now consolidated their predecessors' domestic successes and expanded outward, determined to make their empire the one and only power in eastern Asia.

This was still a turbulent age; frontiers needed defending against hostile tribes, and internal order at times collapsed. At the midpoint of the dynasty, the line of Han monarchs was briefly broken, when Wang Mang, a member of another aristocratic house—who had been acting as regent to an infant emperor—usurped the throne. His 14 years of rule (from AD 9 to 23) came to an end when the Han managed to regain their power. But however brief Wang Mang's reign may have been, historians use it as a demarcation point to separate what they refer to as the Early, or Western, Han, from the Later, or Eastern, Han.

Despite the upheavals of the age, the Han Chinese, like their Roman contemporaries, created a way of life that would leave its imprint upon successive generations for the better part of the next 2,000 years. The period had its wise and foolish monarchs, cruel tyrants, and enlightened philosopher-kings. It had as well its bureaucrats and lawmakers, engineers who flung roads and fortifications across thousands of miles of hitherto untamed territory, and a robust merchant class that sent caravans laden with goods over the many east-west routes that would become known as the Silk Road.

The age also had its poets with their vivid word pictures and their cries from the heart. Perhaps most important of all were its historians—Sima Qian, who composed *Records of the Historian,* and Ban Gu, who wrote *History of the Former Han.* Their lengthy works have been preserved by copyists and scrutinized by Chinese scholars. Now, thanks to an increase in archaeological discoveries that have been made in recent decades, the veracity of the ancient texts can be tested against the evidence of the finds.

Because the Han, like earlier dynasties, espoused the belief

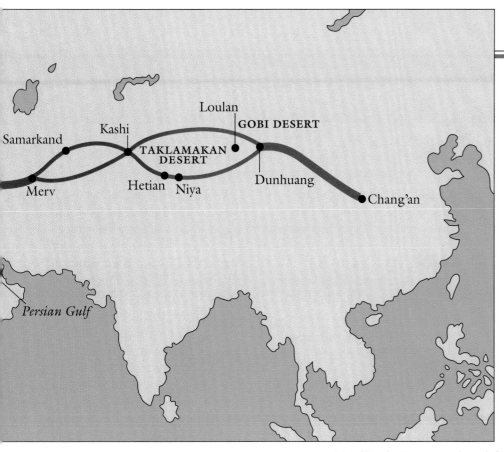

Loulan
Kashi
GOBI DESERT
Samarkand
TAKLAMAKAN
DESERT
Merv
Hetian   Niya
Dunhuang
Persian Gulf
Chang'an

History's most fabled trade artery, the Silk Road split into several byways as it skirted the great Taklamakan Desert and meandered toward the Mediterranean. Traversing the road's 4,000-mile length, camel caravans bore Chinese silks west and Western gold and glass to the east. Few merchants traveled the entire route but rather traded their goods in stages along the way.

that one should "treat the dead as the living," their burial customs provide a revealing legacy. The style in which a person made that final journey reflected the position that he or she had occupied in the world, with its rigid social stratifications.

The poor, accordingly, went to their graves with little or nothing that they could call their own. In 1955 an excavation in Luoyang in Henan Province turned up a Han peasant cemetery where a few coarse pots and the simplest of cheap coffins demonstrated clearly that these were the only parting gifts the mourners could afford. Among the rich and highborn, however, it was a different story. To ensure that the spirits of the affluent or aristocratic dead should dwell happily in the world to come, they were well provided for. As in generations past, grieving heirs endowed their parents' resting places with all manner of practical items and luxury goods: bronze and lacquer vessels, food and drink, furniture, clothing, mirrors and cosmetics, official seals, legal documents, and books written on silk or on bamboo slips.

As time passed, fashions in grave goods changed. Instead of burying treasured possessions—some families were actually becoming impoverished by the funerals that they provided for their parents—Han mourners increasingly began to equip their family tombs with small ceramic sculptures, three-dimensional replicas of houses, farms, and estates, complete with little figures of the people and animals that inhabited them.

Other graphic illustrations of Han life survive on bricks and tiles and on the doorposts and the supporting columns of tombs. In some burials, murals enlivened the walls with reproductions of surroundings once familiar to the deceased.

The artisans of the age set themselves the task of reproducing even the most commonplace features of daily life. And because they did so, they have given modern eyes glimpses of princes in their

119

REVERENCE FOR JADE OF HEAVEN, GUARDIAN AGAINST DECAY

Tough as steel yet translucent, and when polished, exquisitely smooth, jade was prized in China above ivory and gold. It was a possession to take to the grave, as the pictures of King Zhao Mo's tomb (which was found in 1983) here and on the following page show. Known as *yu,* it's name came to connote "precious," "noble," and "pure." Yu is Central Asian nephrite, a white stone tinged with reds or browns. (The more familiar green jade is jadeite, unknown in China until the 17th century AD.)

When used in court ceremonies, the "stone of Heaven" symbolized noble or princely rank. In funeral rituals, it was deemed a fit offering for the gods. The rich

adorned themselves with jade, and Confucius saw in it "all the beauties and virtues of a gentleman," including intelligence, humanity, loyalty, and truth.

Yu was included in burials as early as the fifth millennium BC. In subsequent eras jade came to be regarded as a preventive against decay and was used to plug bodily orifices. Jade cicadas—insects that seemingly return from the dead after a long gestation in the soil—were often placed in corpses' mouths.

Although the Shang dynasty gave rise to the custom of burying the dead with sets of worked jade, the late Zhou and Han periods brought jade carving to a peak of perfection. In 122 BC

Zhao Mo, who had declared himself king of Nanyue, was laid to rest in Guangzhou wearing a jade suit and surrounded by more than 200 objects made from the mineral as well. This renegade had defied the Han ban on human sacrifice to have himself buried with four wives, five cooks, and an entertainer. But despite his precious suit, Zhao Mo decayed, leaving behind only traces of his bones amid his rich cache of indestructible jade.

One of the earliest of several dozen jade burial suits found, this one belonged to King Zhao Mo. Restored, it consists of 2,291 rough-hewn plaques that are glued onto cloth and linked by red silk ribbons. Normal practice called for the pieces to be wired together.

When it was opened in 1983, Zhao Mo's rock-cut burial chamber had lain undisturbed for 2,100 years. Viewed from the foot of his now vanished coffin (only the bronze handles remain), his jade suit lies in pieces with jade disks once massed atop and beneath the self-styled king's body. Near the head pieces of Zhao Mo's suit archaeologists found a fine, openwork jade plaque (above) depicting a dragon. On the beast's ankle stands a scolding phoenix, whose scrolling crest and tail fill the outer band.

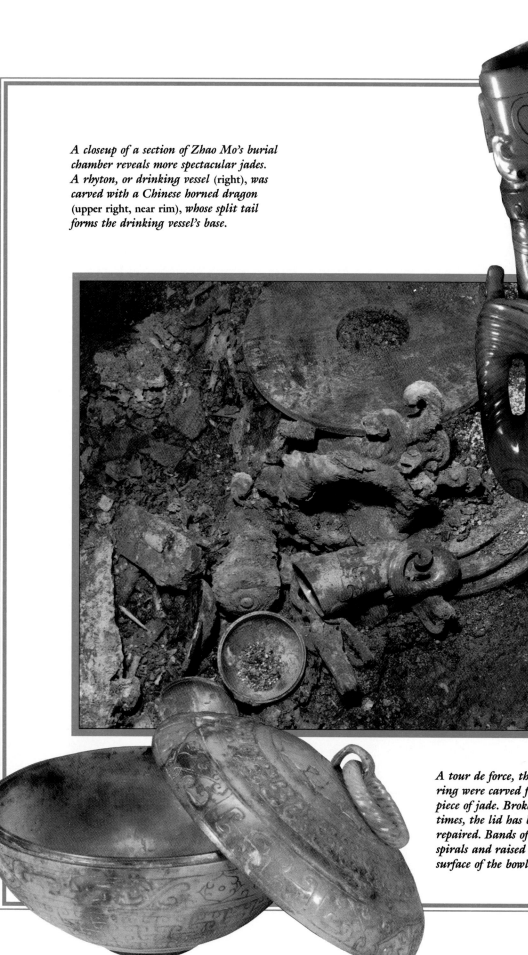

A closeup of a section of Zhao Mo's burial chamber reveals more spectacular jades. A rhyton, or drinking vessel (right), was carved with a Chinese horned dragon (upper right, near rim), whose split tail forms the drinking vessel's base.

A tour de force, this bowl's lid and ring were carved from a single piece of jade. Broken in ancient times, the lid has been meticulously repaired. Bands of interlocking spirals and raised dots cover the surface of the bowl.

palaces, soldiers on patrol, artisans in their workshops, peasants in the fields, and pigs and poultry feeding in the mud beneath a domestic privy. The result of these artistic endeavors—and of the society's attention to the honors due the deceased—has been to put flesh on the bones of written history and to open up a window into the vigorous world of the Han dynasty.

The man destined to become the first Han emperor was Liu Bang, a soldier from a humble family. Later chroniclers described him as a formidable warrior with a thrusting nose, a "dragon forehead," a fine beard, and a left thigh marked with 72 black moles, considered an auspicious number. His military career began late in the third century BC, in the dying days of the Qin dynasty, when rebel armies and bandit gangs rose up to overthrow their tyrannical ruler. A natural leader, Liu Bang became the general of the rebel forces. He was a master strategist and a bold commander in the field but no intellectual. Indeed, according to one account, he bore a passionate hatred for scholars. During the revolt, when a delegation of cap-and-gown-clad Confucian sages arrived at his headquarters to give him the benefit of their wisdom, Liu Bang lost his temper, snatched the cap off one of the learned heads, and urinated into it.

What Liu Bang lacked in etiquette, however, he compensated for by his practical abilities. He defeated not only the Qin forces but his major rival for power as well, a man under whom Liu Bang had previously served in the field. Then he set up a new capital, at Chang'an, near modern Xi'an in Shaanxi Province. There he enthroned himself as emperor, declaring he was the Son of Heaven.

His fledgling dynasty faced prodigious challenges. The breaches in the body politic, legacy of the turmoil caused by the overthrow of the Qin, had to be mended. The new emperor distributed great tracts of land to his trusted followers as feudal holdings, and his successors made their sons and kinsmen into kings of the far-flung regions of the realm.

To bind all of these separate fiefdoms together, the central government relied on a hierarchy of officials, whose positions were based on their ability to pass examinations, not so much on social or family connections. Promising young men were recruited from all parts of the realm, talent spotted by provincial bureaucrats. Once they were appointed, these civil servants enjoyed the benefits of a meritocratic career structure, with regular promotions and badges of rank—gold, silver, or bronze seals from which hung ribbons of purple, blue, yellow, or black, denoting position and salary. An imperial edict of 144 BC, promulgated by Liu Sheng's father, proclaimed, "Now the officials are the teachers of the people. It is proper that their carriages, their clothes and robes, should correspond to their dignity." These worthies carried their marks of status to their graves. Excavations of their tombs have yielded lists of their posts and promotions, their treasured seals of office, and their libraries of books written on silk or on bamboo slips.

Under the supervision of these professionals, the government could undertake extraordinary programs of social engineering as deemed necessary for defense or the economy or in times of flood or famine. The inhabitants of overpopulated districts, rich and poor alike, were summarily transferred or deported to emptier regions ripe for cultivation. As many as two million people found themselves uprooted and resettled on the northern frontiers to help increase the security of their borders.

Such far-reaching plans were made in the imperial capital, Chang'an, the hub of the Han universe. (In the first century AD, after the coup that interrupted dynastic continuity, the Han emperors moved the capital to Luoyang, in the shadow of the Mang Mountains.) Excavations at Chang'an have revealed that wooden bridges crossed a moat that ran around the city's perimeter, leading to 12 gates—three on each side—through walls of rammed earth that rose about 40 feet high. These fortifications enclosed an area of 13 square miles, containing the palaces of the imperial family, storehouses, government offices, a state armory, as well as the simple shelters of the humble and the mansions of the rich. A few aristocrats resided close to the palace, while the ordinary people lived farther out in the northern sector. Within their palaces, Han emperors dwelled in relative seclusion, maintaining their status by separation from the mundane world. Their companions were slaves, trusted eunuchs, and the ladies of the court—consorts, concubines, and mothers.

The liveliest parts of the towns, and undoubtedly the noisiest, were the marketplaces. According to contemporary chroniclers, Chang'an boasted nine, each of which had its own team of government officials to supervise commercial activities. One first-century AD writer claimed that, amid the bustle of fruit vendors, fortune-tellers, herbalists, and hawkers, there was no room to turn one's head, let alone maneuver a cart full of produce. Shoppers enjoyed occasional diversions, since the marketplace was also the site for edifying public executions, when convicted criminals lost their heads or were cut in half by the state executioner.

Archaeologists excavating Chang'an, from the 1950s to the 1970s, found large quantities of molds for coins, indicating not only that the cash economy was well established by the Early Han but also that the metal tokens that fueled its transactions were manufactured close to the commercial centers where they would begin their journeys from hand to hand.

For those fortunate individuals whose coffers were full of these useful bits of metal, life offered an almost endless round of pleasures. The tombs of the well-to-do unearthed by modern archaeologists contain ample evidence of these delights and recreations: Ceramic entertainers juggle, cavort, beat drums, perform acrobatics, or dance to the soundless music of miniature orchestras playing panpipes, bells, and zithers. One wall painting shows cooks in meticulously organized kitchens preparing the delicacies for a banquet of many courses. In relief-modeled pleasure gardens and parks, shrubs and flowers perfume the air, ponds provide multicolored carp, birds sing, and exotic animals prowl.

Digs in the Han capitals, plus the replicas of buildings found in graves, have helped modern scholars piece together a picture of the ancient townscape. The palaces, which boasted towered gateways, were constructed of timber, with plastered walls painted white or scarlet. Among the ruins of the palaces, archaeologists found scattered semicircular roof tiles. Some obviously had projected out over the eaves, for they had been sealed with circular end pieces for decorative purposes. These relics, like the ceramic sculptures and the wall paintings in the tombs, shed light on the preoccupations of their original owners. Some of them bore simple designs, such as a cloud pattern, while others offered a prayer for eternal happiness or even a quasi-political declaration. "Heaven has brought about the foreigners' submission," announced one such tile found near a troubled northern frontier; while another broadcast to any passing invader the warning, "All aliens surrender."

The rich and noble lived in capacious houses, arranged around courtyards and galleried pavilions. The interiors were furnished with richly carved woodwork, while woolen rugs or woven matting covered the floors. The residents preserved their privacy with screens. Although the houses have vanished, the comfortable style of the owners' lives is evoked by their tombs.

In the 1970s archaeologists came across three tombs at Mawangdui—a site located not far from Changsha in Hunan Province—which belonged to the marquis of Dai, who died around 186 BC, his wife, the marquise, and their son. Although the marquis's tomb had been extensively damaged by water, the other two were intact and provided extraordinary insights into the Han world. Mother and son, who died within a few months of each other some 18 years after the marquis, had been interred with a number of objects from everyday life. The marquise's possessions were in a remarkable state of preservation. In spite of the presence of considerable moisture, her son's tomb yielded a cache of important copies of manuscripts written in ink on silk and stored in bamboo hampers.

These texts, comprising 120,000 Chinese characters, afford modern scholars an opportunity to study works of history, geography, medicine, astronomy, and philosophy set down more than two millennia ago. Among the manuscripts is the oldest surviving version of the *Daodejing (The Way and the Power)*, the basic work of Daoism—a philosophy that had developed during the Warring States period—including sections that had been lost over time. A treatise on astronomy showed heavenly constellations and revealed theoretical knowledge of at least five planets—Venus, Jupiter, Mercury, Mars, and Saturn. There was even a work devoted to physical regimens, with 40 illustrations of exercises that were accompanied by text explaining that the movements were based on those of animals and going on to describe proper breathing control.

Dying shortly after her son, the marquise of Dai was interred near him, in a tomb that yielded, in addition to more than a thousand grave gifts, the miraculously preserved body of the deceased herself *(pages 145-157)*, still moist and supple after its 2,100-year interment. To ensure that her happiness in the afterlife would be

Complete with courtyard, gatehouse, and looming watchtower, this 28-inch-tall clay model from a tomb in Hubei Province depicts an elaborate manor house typical of those that dominated the estates of the wealthy and formed the social and economic hubs of Han rural life.

complete, her mourners had provided a variety of foods, lists of dishes, and even recipes.

If the Han rich dined well, it was because there were millions of people who toiled at the base of the social pyramid to grow the crops that fed the empire. "Agriculture is the foundation of the world," pronounced one Early Han emperor, promulgating a decree on the thorny subject of taxing grain, "No duty is greater."

As the emperor knew, the wealth of his realm depended on the success of its farmers' harvests. The vast majority of the population broke down into family units of four or five people, who worked small plots that were sometimes their own but more often the property of landlords capable of demanding as much as half the harvest in rent. The ownership of land was not taken lightly; some Han landlords insisted that their graves be furnished with copies of leases, ensuring their rights, for all eternity, to the ground where they lay.

The most important crops on any farm were the grains that formed the base, and the bulk, of the Chinese diet—wheat, millet, barley, and beans in the heartlands of northern China, rice farther south—and hemp, whose fiber was used to make garments. Anyone who could afford it tried to keep a pig or some chickens, but meat provided only a small and occasional part of the average peasant diet.

Those farming in the precarious peace of the borderlands sometimes had to double as soldiers. Some estates in frontier districts were run as military colonies, with army units posted there specifically to labor in the fields.

In 1972 the six-room tomb of a wealthy second-century AD colonel was excavated at Helingeer in Inner Mongolia. It was lined with more than 50 scenes, many of peasants at work on his country estate. Some of the colorful murals revealed that the colonel had found it necessary to erect fortifications and a watchtower to defend his manor. Peace reigned at Helingeer, however, at least at the hypothetical moment frozen in time by the tomb's muralist. The colonel is shown entertaining his guests with jugglers, musicians, and dancers, while a vast coterie of servants waits upon the party. Near the cluster of buildings that served as home to the manor's inhabitants, peasants hoe the soil of a vegetable garden, which has been walled off against the incursions of the pigs and the fowls that forage around the pens housing young sheep and oxen.

Because of his estate's location on rich, northern pasture land, the colonel could diversify his efforts, rearing livestock that needed grazing room and still managing to cultivate grain. One of the murals shows men tilling a large field with ox-drawn plows. Elsewhere, the oxcarts stand ready to carry the gathered harvest to the granaries, and laborers busy themselves winnowing the grain. In yet another mural, workers can be seen netting clumps of hemp in a pool, where the vegetable matter surrounding the fibers would disintegrate in the water, freeing the fibers for spinning or twisting into rope. The colonel had also tried his hand at silk cultivation. Four women, equipped with ropes and hooks, stand in a grove of mulberry trees, gathering the leaves that hold the silkworms in order to transfer them to nearby bamboo baskets.

These activities would have been familiar sights to a provincial governor named Cui Shi, who also lived in the second century AD. Scion of a once-wealthy family that had fallen on hard times, he spent the last of his inheritance in paying for his father's funeral ceremonies and struggled to recoup these losses by working in the socially stigmatized liquor trade. In order to restore some of the family's honor, Cui Shi accepted an unglamorous official posting as the governor of Wuyuan in Inner Mongolia.

There Cui Shi sought to alleviate the miseries of the peasantry by setting up a modest textile industry. The governor was surprised to discover that the populace knew very little about weaving. They had nothing but rough garments made of local grasses to shield them from the bitter winds blowing out of Mongolia.

In another attempt to help out the struggling farmers, Cui Shi wrote a slim volume on agriculture, which still survives in fragmentary form. The governor of Wuyuan's text provides information on the proper observation of religious festivals, the making of simple medicines, the education of the young, and the care and maintenance of livestock, house-

From the shaded elegance of a chariot drawn by a prancing steed, a wealthy Han army colonel turned landowner and his driver set out to view his extensive property and ample flocks. The walled manor house in this painting from his six-room tomb suggests the need for vigilance. The peasant farmers who worked the estate also constituted its militia.

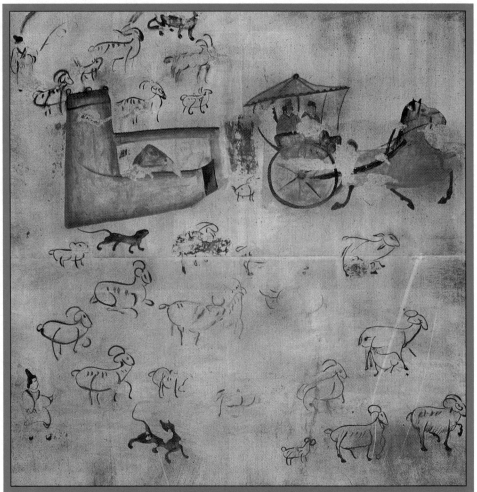

Bowed by the weight of both his task and his social status, a peasant pours out his quota of grain for a tax collector seated with bamboo tally slips in hand. This Later Han stamped brick from a tomb found in 1974 in Sichuan Province contrasts the functionary's luxurious robes with the meager garb of the rural poor.

hold utensils, and field tools. Cui Shi also provided a suitable schedule for the year's work on the farm, explaining the right months for breaking up heavy ground and lighter soils, for hay cutting and hoeing, for sowing vegetables, and for gathering healing herbs.

Farmers' wives were instructed by Cui Shi in keeping a calendar of their own. There was a correct season for breeding silkworms to achieve threads of suitable strength and quality and a time for textile spinning, washing old clothes and sewing new ones, sandal making, brewing, and preserving fresh foods for winter use. And for the edification of both men and women, Cui Shi designated a month when cosmic influences dictated that husbands and wives could best guard their health and happiness if they went to bed in separate rooms.

A much earlier Han agricultural author, who had the advantage of the emperor's ear at court, was the second-century BC reformer Zhao Guo. He encouraged new tools and more efficient methods for working the land. Instead of the old wooden single plow, he advocated the use of the more efficient iron double plowshare, pulled by a pair of oxen or—if necessary—a pair of men. And, to prevent the costly loss of seed, he urged farmers to abandon the practice of scattering it over six-foot-wide strips of ground. Instead, he encouraged them to divide these strips into three shallow furrows and to walk along the ridges to drop the precious kernels into the indentations in regular lines. Output may have been enhanced even further by another invention—a seed drill composed of several small iron tubes. As it was pulled along by oxen, the drill inserted the seed into the earth at regular intervals and at a depth favorable to growth.

For many Han farmers, the most dramatic improvement in their prospects came through the mass production of iron tools. The number of privately owned iron foundries proliferated in the second century BC, and by 100 BC the government had established foundries in most provinces, eventually bringing the production of the metal—as well as of that other equally vital substance salt—under its own monopolistic control. Forty-eight state foundries began turning out agricultural tools, cooking pots, weapons, components for ox-carts, and other specialized goods in huge, new coal-fired blast fur-

naces built of heat-resistant brick. One of the most impressive of these was the foundry of Tieshenggou, Gongxian, in Henan Province, where archaeologists have excavated 21,527 square feet of the site, revealing 18 furnaces for separating iron from ore, others for casting at higher temperatures, still others for making steel. Some of the Han furnaces were capable of producing as much as a ton a day of the iron after the introduction of the twin-action piston bellows, which provided a continual blast of air. The human labor that was originally used to activate these bellows was replaced by hydraulic energy in the Later Han period, in the form of a horizontal waterwheel powered by river currents.

Tools, or images of them, discovered in hundreds of tombs indicate that the Han Chinese used laborsaving devices that would not make their way to the fields of the Han's European counterparts for a thousand years or more. Farmers, in particular, reaped the benefit of these inventions.

The wheelbarrow, which would not make its way west until the 11th or 12th century AD, began easing the burdens of Han laborers soon after 100 BC. Chroniclers of that time told tales of a holy man from Sichuan Province, in southwestern China, who built himself—as they put it—a wooden goat or sheep and used it to ride into the mountains. A tomb dating from around AD 100 contains a frieze showing a man sitting on a clearly recognizable wheelbarrow; another barrow, decorating a slightly later tomb, is depicted in action, with someone pushing it. By the end of the Han dynasty, the wheelbarrow became commonplace and was popularly known as a "wooden ox" or "gliding horse."

The pounding of grain was rendered easier by pedal-driven hammers, and crank-handled fans winnowed the kernels from the chaff. It would take some 1,800 years before Dutch sailors on the East Indies run and French Jesuits visiting China brought this ingenious winnowing machine back to the West. Almost as great an

130

interlude would be required before another vital Chinese invention found its way westward—the circulating chain pump, used to lift square pallets laden with earth or water. The chain pump was first mentioned by a Chinese philosopher in a text dated AD 80 and was used by second-century engineers to carry water into the Eastern Han capital city of Luoyang. Some 1,400 years later, the first European versions of the pumps appeared, copied faithfully from the Chinese.

Other innovations, less directly connected to the land, also emerged from Han burials. Rudders, making it possible to steer a ship with much greater accuracy than oars could provide, were first seen on Han Chinese vessels. A pottery model of one craft, found in a first-century AD tomb, boasts a rudder that could be raised on ropes or chains to protect it from damage in the shallows. In the West, rudders did not appear until the early Middle Ages.

Most of the histories that described these early Chinese inventions were written on silk or on bamboo slips; their authors did not yet appreciate the significance of what would become the most important invention for their own craft, paper. The world's earliest surviving sample was discovered in a tomb in Shaanxi Province in 1957. Its raw material was hemp fiber. Archaeologists have dated the fragment to the period between 140 and 87 BC.

The scrap, as it happens, is blank. It would be another century or so before the Chinese would turn to paper as a medium for writing. In the interim, they would use it for clothing—early samples were thick and coarse enough to provide an almost suffocating degree of insulation—or, occasionally, for hygienic purposes. A text written in 93 BC notes that a palace guard advised a prince to cover his nose with a piece of paper, perhaps to shield him from noxious vapors, if not to catch an actual sneeze. Legal documents regarding a murder case in 12 BC indicate that the poison used in the killing had been conveyed in a little parcel of red paper.

But by the beginning of the next century, words began to be written on the medium. When a troop of imperial soldiers abandoned its watchtower during a tribal uprising, it left behind a note bearing about two dozen faded but decipherable characters, which was buried when the fortress fell. In 1942, during warfare on a considerably larger scale, someone searching through the ancient ruins found the nearly 2,000-year-old message.

Those who derived the greatest benefits from these new materials, tools, conveniences, and techniques were not necessarily the people who produced the goods but those who bought and sold them—traders and merchants, moneylenders, and entrepreneurs. The historian Sima Qian quoted a piece of contemporary wisdom that would hold as true for other ages and cultures as it would for the Han: "When men have no wealth at all, they live by their brawn; when they have a little, they struggle to get ahead by their brains; and when they already have plenty of money, they look for an opportunity for a good investment. This in general is the way things work."

Sima Qian cited the success story of a lowly official named Ren, who was in charge of a local granary during the period of chaos between the overthrow of the old Qin dynasty and the resumption of order under the Han. The presence of rival armies trampling over their fields had kept the local farmers from planting crops in the proper season. Sensing that hard times lurked just around the corner, Ren buried the grain from his storehouse in a hole in the ground and waited. Soon, with nothing to harvest, the price of grain shot up beyond all reckoning, and famine loomed. A large portion of hoarded gold and jewels found its way into Ren's coffers in exchange for his now far more precious grain. But unlike other war profiteers, Ren and his family lived frugally, saved their resources, consumed only what their own fields and herds produced, and bought up all the best land in the district, ensuring the wealth of his descendants for several generations to come.

The merchant, especially when he followed the example of Ren and converted profits into land, had become an economic force to be reckoned with. But those who lived by their wits and business acumen were not highly regarded even by the people who queued up to purchase the wares. In the eyes of the aristocrats, scholars, and court officials who constituted the Han elite, there was little distinction to be made between the shopkeeper selling salt out of sacks in the market and the budding industrialist with a thousand slaves at his disposal digging into the earth for iron ore.

From the early years of the dynasty, laws were passed to curb the extravagances of the newly rich and keep them in their place. In 199 BC, for instance, the emperor issued an edict announcing that "merchants are not to be permitted to wear brocade, embroidery, flowered silk, crepe linen, sackcloth or wool, carry weapons, or ride in a chariot or on a horse."

It was hard for those with money to resist the temptation to spend it, for the people of this era loved beautiful things as much as

their ancestors had and demanded a high level of workmanship. The artisans who supplied the wares were often required to inscribe their names on each piece, so that they could be held accountable for quality. A lacquered cup from the first century AD, for instance, bore an incised inscription around its base, identifying the workshop where it was made, its capacity, and the individuals who had taken part in its production: "Sized by Jin; lacquered by Ji; final coat by [Qin]; handles gilded by [Mao]; painted by Li; engraved by Yi; cleaned and polished by Zheng; checked by Yi; officer commanding the factory guard, Zhang; director, Liang; deputy director, Feng; assistant, Long; scribe, Bao."

Most of the glories of the Han, however, were produced by

Acrobats, dancers, and musicians entertain officals wearing court dress who line both sides of this 27-inch-long ceramic tableau. Unearthed from a first- or second-century BC grave in Shandong Province, the piece recalls the elaborate musical revels that enlivened the banquets of Han subjects well enough off to afford such entertainment.

those whose names have been lost. Not even the lowliest social outcasts could escape recruitment into the grand schemes of their imperial masters. How the ordinary folk lived was a matter of little interest to their well-off contemporaries so long as they could enjoy the fruits of the commoners' labor. Fortunately archaeology has shed some light on these people and their anonymous efforts.

For years, during the first half of the 20th century, the farmers of Yanshi Xian in Henan Province working the land at a place named Xidajiaocun had called the area "the Ditch of Skeletons." Here human bones sprouted from the yellow soil as readily as any planted crop—so too, from time to time, did fragments of broken brick with puzzling inscriptions. Those that scholars could decipher bore references to shackles, punishments, and prisons.

In 1964 a team of Chinese archaeologists began to investigate the source of this harvest of bones. They uncovered a cemetery dating from the early second century AD, containing the shallow graves of prisoners who had died while serving sentences of forced labor. The convicts had been working on construction projects at the capital of Luoyang, whose ruins lay about a mile from the excavation site. The cemetery covered an area of 41,800 square yards. Only 1,672 square yards were excavated, but even that small portion yielded more than 500 graves. Long rows of the narrow, rectangular pits stretched out in all directions.

Alongside each of the skeletons, the excavators found one or two bricks conveying such information as the name of the work gang to which the prisoner had belonged, the prison from which the convict had come, and the penalty imposed for the crime. The prisoner was identified as one who was either compelled to work in chains or was exempt from this added restriction on movement. Note was taken of any skills that might have made the worker particularly useful to the project at hand. Some of the graves gave testimony of a more generous tribute, where some witness to the burial had tossed in a few small coins.

Most of the remains were male, but the bodies of several female prisoners were uncovered. The members of both sexes had, for the most part, died young; their bones showed signs of extraordinary wear and tear. Some Chinese scholars believe the overseers had pushed the prisoners beyond endurance. Death must

LUSTROUS TREASURES MADE OF SAP

The ancient and exquisite art of lacquering constitutes one of China's premier contributions to the world of craftsmanship. Many fine examples have turned up in tombs, but few in more wondrous condition than the trove of perfectly preserved objects—including the gleaming black and red vessel with pouring spout pictured below— that had lain undisturbed for 2,100 years within a side compartment of the marquise of Dai's tomb *(pages 145-157),* until its excavation in 1972. Along with the lady's gorgeously lacquered nested coffins, the dishes, bowls, and other containers typify the highest achievements of a demanding craft that originated as far back as the Neolithic period in China.

As in the past, the sap of the lacquer tree, indigenous to East Asia, is still tapped from the trunk, heated, and purified, then applied to a base form that can be made of wood, leather, ceramic, or metal, in dozens of infinitesimally thin coats. In ancient times even sword sheaths, shields, and parts of carriages were coated with lacquer because of its protective properties. Properly dried and sanded, the layers of resin give items a smooth sheen, as well as durability, lacquer being impervious to water, acid, heat, and such insects as termites. The resin itself is a dull gray, but when colors—at first cinnabar red, carbon black, and by Han times blue, green, yellow, silver, and gold—are added to the substance, a lacquered product will all but glow. That effect can be heightened by carving the piece's boldly hued surface or inlaying it with shell or bone, as was done during the Shang period, or with silver and gold, as during the Eastern Zhou and the Han.

For all its apparent technical simplicity, however, the art of lacquering as practiced in China demanded extraordinary amounts of time and labor. Each of the numerous coats required skilled and delicate application, and each of them took days to dry. As many as 200 layers of lacquer might be applied when an object's surface was to be carved. Painting intricate decorations in the viscous lacquer called for exceptional control of the brush. Because many artisans collaborated to fashion each item and the process was so lengthy, lacquerware was extremely costly—in Han times perhaps 10 times as valuable as a similar piece in bronze. Despite the high price, though, the ware's great practicality and durability, as well as its beauty, made for high demand. Eventually the government became involved in the production of this precious but lucrative commodity and by the first or second year AD was sponsoring at least three factories.

have been a familiar visitor to the work camp, for some of the graves showed signs of having been turned over and dug up after a few years in order to make room for others. Even in the afterlife, a convict could not hope to rest in peace.

A larger prisoner graveyard was unearthed eight years later near the great unopened mausoleum of the second-century BC emperor Jing. Excavations in 1990, adjacent to his tomb, would dazzle the world, revealing pits that contained hundreds of lifelike, doll-size soldiers, formed from terra cotta *(pages 138-139)*. The care with which this army was memorialized did not, however, extend to those miserable souls who had died in the process of digging the pits in which the figures were positioned row upon row and constructing the underground chambers that housed them. For nearby, on a 66,880-square-yard site, lay the grisly remains of an estimated 10,000 unfortunate individuals. Many of them had iron fetters still clamped to their necks or their ankles. They lay in single graves or had been flung into communal pits.

The discovery of these burial places confirmed the accounts of ancient Chinese chroniclers who had written of the convict-labor brigades at work on Emperor Jing's tomb. Ban Gu's *History of the Former Han,* for instance, reported that "prisoner-laborers who constructed the [tomb] were pardoned from the death penalty." But the teams of workers uncovered near the emperor's tomb did not consist only of convicted criminals. Mingled among their remains were the bones of honest men and women, some of whom had been civilian conscripts drafted by official edict to serve for five years on public-works projects, others impoverished peasants who had sold themselves into work gangs after being bankrupted by bad harvests or by cold-hearted landlords.

These toilers, and the hundreds of thousands like them in graves as yet unopened, provided the labor for the dynasty. They were the people who built the palaces that housed the mighty Han emperors in life and the opulent monuments that sheltered them in death. The workers paid with their sweat and blood for the tamped-earth defensive walls that ran for hundreds of miles along the western borders, for the metals mined from the earth, for the roads that eased communications between all corners of the expanding state, and for the dikes that guarded communities from catastrophic floods.

Surviving Han chronicles recount the massive efforts marshaled toward one such program of flood control. In 109 BC tens of thousands of conscript laborers dug, heaved, and hauled earth, at the behest of Emperor Wu, to stanch a great rupture in a dike on the Yellow River. To spur these draftees in their efforts, the monarch himself made a personal visit to the site and read them a poem he had written for the great occasion. Whatever the literary merits of this work, its imperial author is now remembered as the Han dynasty's greatest ruler and the most vigorous defender of the realm.

The Han emperor Wu ruled China from 141 to 87 BC, and his reign saw the armies at their busiest. Looking southward, the Han went on the offensive—pacifying, colonizing, and opening the way for trade. Merchants and soldiers, in their separate but equally persuasive ways, began the work of bringing hitherto alien southern regions, such as Guangzhou (Canton), under the control of the Han. Gradually they succeeded in extending the reach of the expanding Chinese empire as far as Vietnam. Its goods traveled even farther through southeast Asia; pieces of Han pottery have turned up at sites in Java, Sumatra, and Borneo.

To the north and west, nomadic tribes—old enemies, whose incursions had impelled the Qin to build defensive "long walls"— looked ever more hungrily toward the prosperous farmlands in the basin of the Yellow River. Most formidable among them were the Xiongnu, who controlled Mongolia. These fierce warriors may have been the ancestors of the Huns, according to some modern scholars. To counter this menace, Emperor Wu conscripted a massive labor force to construct new walls, gates, and watchtowers and to rebuild old defenses. Expeditionary troops, numbering more than 100,000 men, marched into the Mongolian steppes.

On the battlefield, the Xiongnu were undoubtedly the superior horsemen, but the Chinese backed up their own less adept cavalry with archers wielding crossbows, an endless supply of mercenaries and conscripts for reinforcements, talented generals, and far superior rations. One Han thinker had suggested that Chinese innkeepers open restaurants right on the border, in sniffing distance of enemy encampments, with delicacies designed to win the hearts, minds, and watering mouths of the barbarians: "When the Xiongnu have developed a craving for our cooked rice, roasted meats, and wine, this will have become their fatal weakness." History does not record whether his advice was heeded.

The reward for Emperor Wu's efforts was to be Han domination of a great swath of Asia, extending into Korea and Man-

churia, with a corridor leading toward the central Asian republics of the former Soviet Union. But the threat of the Xiongnu on the northern and western frontiers would remain throughout the Han dynasty's reign.

In the course of his never-ending struggles against the Xiongnu, Emperor Wu undertook an experiment in foreign diplomacy. Reports had reached him that far to the west lived certain tribes who bore as little love for the Xiongnu as did the Han. On the principle that my enemy's enemy is my friend, the emperor dispatched an envoy, Zhang Qian, to make contact with the tribes. Described by the reign's historian as being a strong-minded extrovert with a generous spirit, Zhang Qian was known to have a knack for getting on well with barbarians.

Row upon row of youthful laborers, some still shackled, most work worn, fill the crowded second-century AD cemetery of Xidajiaocun. Some were buried with a coin or two, others with only a brick epitaph (inset) bearing the prisoner's name, place of origin, and sentence. This one indicates that the victim was condemned to four years' hard labor.

Thirteen years later, when the emperor had presumably given his ambassador up for dead, having heard no word from him, Zhang Qian reappeared with a Xiongnu wife and a remarkable story. He had been captured by the Xiongnu, who had treated him well but held him under surveillance. After 10 years, he gave his captors the slip and continued westward to the land called Bactria, controlled by the nomads known as the Yuezhi. This tribe did indeed have a grievance against the Xiongnu, who had murdered the father of their present chief. But they saw no reason to go to war at the behest of a monarch from some distant land.

Whatever Zhang Qian's private mortification at failing in his mission, his travels held great historic significance. For the emperor's emissary discovered that Chinese goods, if not Chinese people, had

THE EMPEROR JING'S MINIATURE RETINUE

Where the modern highway skirts the burial mound of the Han emperor Jing, not far from his capital city of Chang'an, archaeologists in the spring of 1990 began unearthing rows of terra-cotta figures that had been carefully placed in underground, ceilinged chambers during the ruler's 15-year reign (from 156 to 141 BC).

The 90 male and female effigies that have been excavated stand at less than one-third the height of the vast army of life-size clay soldiers mustered for Qin Shihuangdi's burial in 210 BC *(pages 105-113)*. Emperor Jing's assemblage, also in contrast to the First Emperor's troops, emerged from the ground completely naked and armless, like the two pictured at left and right. Bits of silk and hemp cloth discovered in the soil, however, indicated that they had originally been clothed. The garments, like

the arms that had been fashioned from some perishable material, had moldered away during the 2,100 years the figures lay in the soil.

Shaped in four-part molds, Emperor Jing's retinue displays only 15 different molded facial expressions, unlike the army of the Qin emperor, whose clay troops boast multiple attitudes and hair styles. And only a portion of Emperor Jing's men

Up to their chins in earth for more than two millennia, the terra-cotta figures shown at right await further excavation as one of their number yields up his secrets to modern archaeologists. Apparently undisturbed by looters or by fallen ceilings, these men retain their orderly formation.

138

Specially recruited for the task and supervised by experts from the Shaanxi Institute of Archaeology, local conservators painstakingly piece together shattered soldiers of Emperor Jing's funeral retinue. The man who is fitting head to torso leads the group.

stand in military array. Although it is impossible to say whether regular troops may occupy yet unexplored pits, the soldiers uncovered so far carry out rearguard duties. In one of the 10 excavated pits, detachments march behind carriages, but the grain surrounding them suggests their less than heroic role as guardians of a granary. Elsewhere, a pit filled with cooking utensils and animals denotes a kitchen.

Such apparently pacific activities would seem to imply a society less warlike in behavior than that of the First Emperor of Qin. But the presence of an immense laborers' graveyard, discovered nearby in 1972, testifies to an oppressive society in which thousands of individuals were forced to toil for the

sake of the Han emperor Jing's posthumous grandeur.

The archaeologists' task of interpreting the terra-cotta figures has been complicated by damage inflicted by thieves over the ages and the depredations of time, which together have left a jumble of broken body parts in several pits under collapsed ceilings. A museum, to be built at the site, will display the patiently reassembled figures alongside those that escaped destruction by man and nature.

made the journey already. In the marketplaces of northern Afghanistan, Zhang Qian was amazed at the sight of bamboo and silk cloth that he knew to be from the southwestern provinces of his own native land. Local traders told him that these products had been carried by merchants from a hot, damp land on the banks of a great river, where warriors rode into battle mounted on the backs of elephants. Emperor Wu later learned that a few intrepid traders from the remote southwestern region of Sichuan did indeed know of a sea route to India from Burma.

Enterprising Chinese would soon find their own way west over a road that followed much the same path that ambassador Zhang Qian had taken. Caravans ventured across central Asia, as far as Persia. From Persia, it was only a relatively small step for traders of the area to move Chinese goods on to Judea, on the eastern shore of the Mediterranean Sea. By the first century BC, Chinese silks would be on sale in Rome.

Sima Qian remarked that now "all the barbarians of the distant west craned their necks to the east and longed to catch a glimpse of China." Their money, if not their persons, gradually reached it. By AD 23 the Chinese state would hold enough of Rome's gold for the Roman emperor Tiberius to impose a ban on the wearing of silk by men in an effort to keep the imperial gold reserves from disappearing into the saddlebags of homeward-bound merchants.

As a reward for his pioneering efforts, Zhang Qian received promotion to high office. But not every emissary sent westward by Emperor Wu enjoyed such a happy end to the journey. In 107 BC, in another diplomatic overture, Wu dispatched a princess, to be given as a bride to a nomad chief, hoping this human gift would persuade him to a military alliance. The young woman saw no cause to rejoice in her role as a political pawn. A lament in verse, believed to be written by her and sent back from her place of exile, still survives: "A tent is my house, of felt are my walls," she wrote. "Raw flesh is my food, with mare's milk to drink; always thinking of my own country, my heart is sad within."

As a Han princess, she longed for a home that was likely to have been a royal palace, luxuriously furnished and amply staffed with slaves to supply her needs almost before she thought of them. Yet most women, whether they were princesses or farmers' daughters, were regarded as the second, inferior sex. Peasant girls were often murdered at birth by disappointed parents, while a lady of the upper classes seems to have had little purpose beyond marrying a spouse of suitably impressive social standing and bearing sons to honor him in life and death.

There was one indomitable woman of the second-century AD imperial court, however, who would not be condemned by a woman's subordinate status to a life of passivity and ignorance. Ban Zhao, born in the middle years of the first century AD, was the daughter of an old aristocratic family with strong intellectual inclinations. Her father had been a highly respected historian, and Ban Zhao grew up in a house where learning was prized above all material gains. There she received an impressive education.

Widowed while still comparatively young, Ban Zhao became tutor to the empress and the ladies of the imperial household, instructing them in classical literature, history, astronomy, and mathematics. When not engaged in teaching, Ban Zhao served as the palace's poet, composing commemorative verses for important anniversaries and state occasions. She also became the unofficial court historian to the emperor He.

The work that ensured Ban Zhao's immortality, however, was a text entitled *Lessons for Women*. Its author intended it as a handbook and survival guide for her two daughters. "A man," she asserted in her introduction, "is able to plan his own life but I do grieve that girls just at the age of marriage, at this time, have no training and advice."

The book's initial premise was that young girls should be entitled to the same elementary education that their brothers enjoyed. In order to fulfill her destiny as a wife and a mother, Ban Zhao argued, a woman deserved to be educated. According to the dualities of Chinese philosophy, the man represents yang, the active principle, and the woman yin, the passive, she conceded, but "only to teach men and not to teach women—is that not ignoring the essential relation between them?"

Ban Zhao did not quarrel with the ancient notion that the man's strength should be balanced by the woman's gentleness, that he should control and she should submit. But Ban Zhao insisted on the acknowledgment of a woman's equal worth and advocated mutual tolerance in marriage. "The correct relationship between husband and wife is based on harmony and intimacy, and conjugal love is grounded in proper union."

Courtiers of both sexes were duly impressed. At least one of Ban Zhao's colleagues in the imperial archives directed the wives and daughters of his family to make copies of the work for their personal use and to live by its precepts.

Ban Zhao had still more ambitious scholarly tasks to occupy her in the emperor's library. Her elder brother, Ban Gu, had been busy compiling *History of the Former Han*. This was not only a chronicle of events but also a compendium of the knowledge of the age, encompassing such subjects as mathematics and astronomy. When her brother died, Ban Zhao continued the project herself.

After the death of Emperor He in AD 106, Ban Zhao became the political adviser to his widow, her star pupil, the empress Deng. This formidable empress-dowager had emerged victorious from one of the frequent behind-the-scenes struggles for royal power in which palace women were often pawns and sometimes active participants. Emperor He had failed to name an heir apparent before his death, and the empress, childless, had the right to make this choice. Deng designated as heir an infant, less than four months old, born to one of Emperor He's concubines. When the baby died a few months later, she selected a 12-year-old boy to be heir over his older brother. Although the child reached his majority three years later, the empress-dowager continued to run the government, assigning her brothers to the necessary military duties and refusing to appoint a regent, except for a short term in which her oldest brother filled this post. She ruled until her death in AD 121.

Encouraged by Empress Deng and later Han emperors—who did not share their ancestor's dislike of learned men—the scholars of the last few decades of the dynasty undertook another monumental academic enterprise. In AD 175 they produced a standard version of the works associated with Confucius and his teachings, pooling their prodigious knowledge to create an edition of absolute textual accuracy that would keep the ancient wisdom intact for future generations. The project took eight years to complete, and scribes used some 50 blocks of stone to inscribe the 200,000 carefully checked and authorized characters of the text. According to the chronicles, scholars flocked by the thousands to the imperial city of Luoyang to admire the achievement.

Great literature could be immortalized on stone, but nothing could keep a dynasty from dying. The late second century AD saw mounting turmoil. A succession of weak and underage emperors made it possible for the families connected to the imperial house by

Three staunch mounted warriors, bearing, from left to right, an ax, a halberd, and a lance, stood at the ready among their bronze comrades in arms in the tomb of General Zhang of the Eastern Han. The Han emperor Wu was so impressed by the Central Asian horses these men ride that he imported them and bred them for battle use.

marriage to exercise ever-increasing power behind the scenes. The strong, centralized state that had been the pride of the great emperor Wu now became fragmented; the court and provincial governments fell prey to corruption.

The last Han emperors were putty in the hands of their eunuchs, who were traditionally the most trusted servants of the throne. Over time, these courtiers had waxed fat and wealthy, buying land, acquiring armies of slaves to run private industrial enterprises, and adopting sons to carry on the family name. Furious at the machinations of a class that they despised and aware of the threat to their own power, in AD 189 a coalition of aristocrats and military men slaughtered 2,000 of these upstarts, which threw the court into a state of confusion.

In the countryside, nature had added to the chaos as floods and famine wrought havoc. Along the lower reaches of the Yellow River, bands of wandering peasants were whipped up into a frenzy by three charismatic leaders, the brothers Zhang, who gathered several hundred thousand armed supporters into a quasi-religious cult known as the Yellow Turbans. In AD 184 they rose, captured towns

on the borders of Shandong and Henan provinces, and spread their influence to other regions.

The imperial government virtually collapsed; the only effective power now lay with the generals who had carried out the coup against the eunuchs in AD 189 and waged war against the rebel bands. General Dong Zhuo, known for his excessive cruelty, marched on Luoyang and put Xian, who would be the last of the Han emperors, on the throne. But a few months later, in AD 190, Dong Zhuo's unruly army, which included barbarian fighters, ran amok in the capital, sacked the city, and put it to the torch.

The soldiers burned the imperial library with all its priceless contents. Scholars wept at the loss of so many intellectual treasures; poets such as Wang Can mourned the end of a glorious era. In a series of verse lamentations entitled *The Seven Sorrows,* Wang Can described the miserable aftermath: "The great city of the West sinks into chaos. Tigers and wolves, the ravagers have arrived. I leave our house. No living soul; only whitened bones strew the plain."

Emperor Xian clung to the throne until forced to abdicate in AD 220. When he stepped down, the great era of the Han came to its end. Four hundred years of division would follow its tragic finale. Yet the legacy of the Han would not be lost. Throughout this period, and during the ensuing cycles of strong rule and periodic disruption, scholars preserved and augmented the Han's intellectual heritage, and artists did not cease in their search for perfection. Dynasties might rise and fall, but the empire itself would recover and survive, and the Sons of Heaven—if not the biological descendants of that rough-spoken old soldier Liu Bang—would preside over China's greatness for nearly 2,000 years to come.

A WOMAN OUT OF THE PAST

She was a most fortunate woman. Born at the dawn of the Han dynasty, Lady Xin, marquise of Dai, lived in an age of peace and prosperity. Her husband, Li Cang, the marquis, was prime minister of Changsha, a vast kingdom encompassing most of present-day Hunan. As a member of the newly elevated aristocracy of the Western Han, he amassed great wealth, and his wife enjoyed a life of extraordinary ease.

Lady Xin suffered from chronic ill health. But the perfumed air she breathed was filled with zither music, servants were always on hand to prepare the rich foods she craved, and her smooth skin knew only silk garments. When she died, around her 50th year, her family spared neither effort nor expense to ensure that she would be equally pampered in the afterlife. Her tomb was abundantly stocked with food, clothing, cosmetics, lacquerware, and a fortune in silk fabrics (samples of which appear above and as the backgrounds to the photos on the following pages). And to serve her in death, as their counterparts had in life, 162 servants and musicians carved in wood were buried by her side.

For more than 2,100 years, the marquise and her provisions lay beneath a saddle-shaped mound on the outskirts of her city, Linxiang, modern Changsha. The knoll came to be known as Mawangdui—Prince Ma's Mound—in the mistaken belief that it covered the grave of a 10th-century AD monarch. Not until 1972, when archaeologists were called in to excavate the site before the construction of a hospital destroyed the tumulus, was it discovered that this was the burial place of the Dai family—Li Cang, Lady Xin, and a grown son.

The finds were among the most electrifying in the annals of recent Chinese archaeology—preeminent in understanding Han culture and its luxury-seeking elite. And in the now wizened body of Lady Xin, miraculously well preserved from her modish coiffure to the feet in her silk slippers *(above)*, the 20th century met a compelling emissary from that bygone time.

DESCENT INTO A WELL-SEALED TOMB

Lady Xin died a widow and a bereaved mother sometime after 168 BC, the year her son was buried and 18 years after the death of her husband. Her body was placed in a coffin sheathed in embroidered silk and appliquéd with feathers. A bright, tasseled silk banner, 6½ feet long and held aloft on a bamboo stave, preceded the "spirit carriage" that carried her body on to the plain two miles east of Linxiang. There, next to the hill that covered the graves of her husband and son, a vertical shaft had been sunk 52 feet into the earth. Mourners must have stood on four ledges carved steplike into the sides of the shaft just above where it narrowed into a funnel-shaped, clay-lined pit containing a massive cypress burial vault.

Draped with the funeral banner, the silk-covered coffin was placed inside a second coffin that was fitted into yet a third. The caskets within caskets were nested inside a compartment in the center of the vault. Four additional compartments held the grave goods—meticulously inventoried on 312 slips of bamboo. Five tons of moisture-absorbing charcoal were packed around the vault, and the top was sealed with three feet of additional clay. Hard rammed earth filled the shaft to the surface.

The remarkable state of preservation in which the marquise and the tomb contents were found was evidently due principally to the dense clay, the absorbent charcoal, and the unvarying temperature deep within the earth. Nothing could get in or out of the sealed crypt. Decay-causing bacteria trapped inside quickly died from lack of oxygen. And while destructive groundwater could not penetrate the insulating barriers, neither could ambient moisture—from such sources as the fresh foods and the marquise's cadaver—seep out. The result was a cool, highly humid, and near-sterile environment in which the delicate silks, the fragile lacquerware, and the shrouded body of the lady herself lay untouched by time, neither rotting nor drying to dust.

The cypress planks that divided the burial vault into separate chambers are taken apart (right) to reveal the outermost of the three nested coffins, which measures 8½ feet long and is painted with swirling cloud motifs and mythological figures to keep evil spirits at bay. The 7½-foot-long red-lacquered middle casket (below) is decorated with propitious animals—stags, tigers, dragons, and phoenixes—which were to assist the soul in its journey. Inside was the silk-clad coffin containing the marquise's remains.

Listed on the tomb's inventory of grave goods as a feiyi, or flying garment, the painted, T-shaped silk banner that was draped face down over the lid of the innermost coffin was the first of its kind found and is considered by some to be the tomb's greatest treasure. Among its beautifully drawn polychrome pictures is a scene at the center of the panel (detail, page 148) depicting a bent, elderly woman that is likely a portrait of the marquise. Precise interpretations of the banner's rich iconography differ, but it is generally agreed that the painting represents an ancient view of the cosmos, with the underworld at the bottom and heaven above, opening its gates to receive the deceased into the spirit world.

A flat-topped, man-made mound more than 13 feet high tops the shaft leading to the burial pit, lined 3 to 4 feet deep in white clay. A layer of charcoal 15 to 19 inches thick surrounds the cypress burial vault, standing more than 9 feet high, 22 feet long, and 16 feet wide. Inside is a chamber for the coffins and four compartments for grave goods.

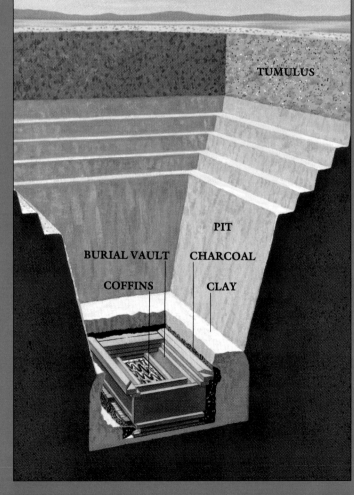

TUMULUS

PIT

BURIAL VAULT

CHARCOAL

COFFINS

CLAY

RESULTS OF A TWENTIETH-CENTURY AUTOPSY

The marquise of Dai's body survived 21 centuries of interment with few signs of decomposition. Her skin was smooth and pliant, her joints were mobile, and her hair was firmly rooted in her scalp. Her internal organs were in such perfect condition that an autopsy produced a detailed medical history.

Just five feet tall, the marquise was an overweight woman in her fifties with type A blood, who had borne children early in life. A bout with tuberculosis had left her lungs scarred, and she was plagued with gallstones, intestinal parasites, and the ache of an old, poorly set fracture in her right arm. A degenerated disk in her lower back had deformed her spine and doubtless made walking painful. Most serious of all, she had advanced atherosclerosis—the narrowing of the arteries that doctors today associate with the fatty diet and sedentary lifestyle of 20th-century industrialized society.

It seems that the marquise, not unlike an overweight, out-of-shape modern executive, dined too well and exercised too little. Her left coronary artery—the principal vessel that supplies oxygen to the heart—was almost totally blocked. Packets of herbal medicine found in the tomb indicate that her physicians had prescribed cinnamon, magnolia bark, and peppercorns for the life-threatening condition. But these traditional remedies for heart disease—still prescribed by Chinese herbalists—were evidently to no avail. "No doubt about it," declared American cardiologist Tsung O. Cheng, who studied the marquise's autopsy reports in 1973. "The lady died of a heart attack."

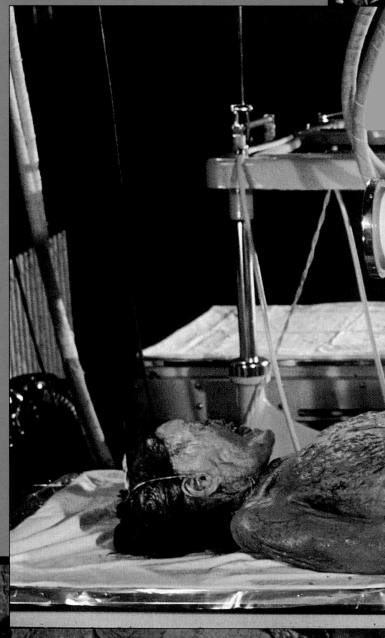

In a scene from Lady Xin's funeral banner, three deferential attendants look on as kneeling servants offer the aged marquise food. The bent back is consistent with the medical evidence of age-induced spinal deformity. Found in the tomb was the walking stick on which the marquise leaned.

The marquise was laid in a coffin wrapped in 20 layers of silk fabric and robes secured on the outside with nine silk ribbons (right). The neatly tied bundle was covered with two quilts, one of yellow gauze, the other of deep red silk embroidered in patterns symbolizing longevity.

The supine corpse is x-rayed at Hunan Medical College where experts from across China came to examine the 2,100-year-old remains. One hundred and thirty-eight musk-melon seeds were recovered from Lady Xin's esophagus, stomach, and intestines, indicating that she died suddenly, soon after eating a large piece of melon.

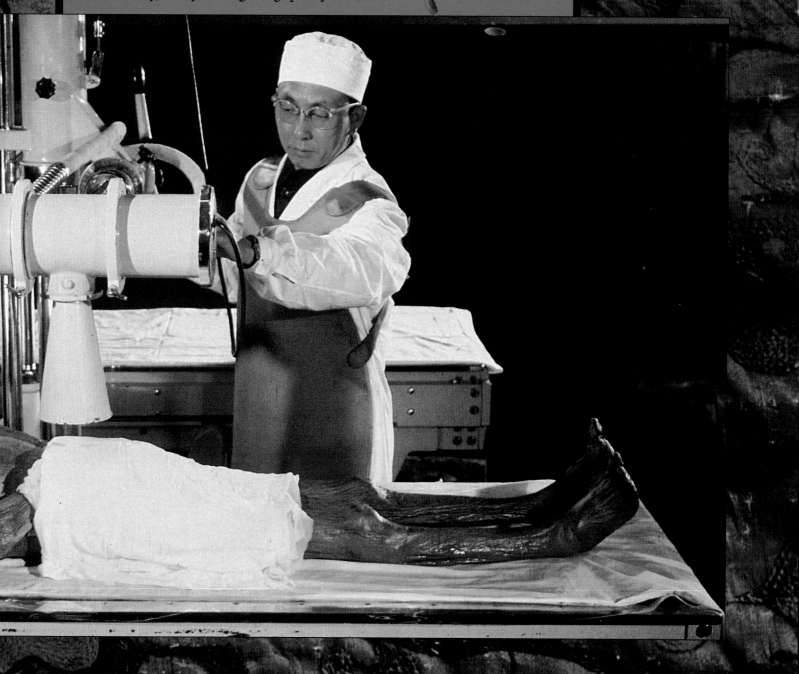

GARMENTS MADE FROM FLOATING MIST

By edict of the thrifty emperor Wen, it was prohibited in Lady Xin's day to bury gold, bronze, or silver with the dead. Accordingly her tomb contained no precious metals. But its treasure in textiles, to say nothing of its lacquerware, was more than sufficient evidence of the Dai family's wealth and position.

By the second century BC, the Chinese had been raising silkworms and spinning their cocoons into cloth for more than 1,000 years. China had a monopoly on silk production, and silk was a medium of exchange, used to pay taxes, tribute, and the salaries of military officers. The rich reveled in it, dressing from the skin out in silk garments, sleeping between silk sheets, draping their homes in silk tapestries, and wrapping everything from medicines to musical instruments in the fabric.

The aristocracy's voracious appetite for silk was fed by legions of silk workers—from solitary rural weavers to laborers in government-run mills. Their prodigious output represented a staggering expenditure in labor. Just one dress length of silk chain-stitched in a pattern such as the swirling longevity design on the sample reproduced here would have taken a skilled embroiderer months to complete.

The more than 100 well-preserved silk items in the marquise's tomb—a cache of ancient Chinese textiles against which all prior finds paled—constituted a broad sampler of Han silk technology, a virtuoso display of weaving, dying, sewing, and fabric-embellishing techniques. The fabrics ranged from "floating mist" gauzes as weightless as a dragonfly's wing to heavy polychrome brocades. There were crepes and damasks, taffetas and twills.

The marquise's tomb held a complete wardrobe, including underwear, nightdresses, coats, robes, skirts, gloves, slippers, and socks. In addition, there were 46 rolls of uncut silk fabric—enough to keep generations of tailors and seamstresses busy stitching up new clothes for her in the afterlife.

The marquise's grave goods lie as they were found when the tomb chamber and all but the innermost coffin (covered with the silk funeral banner) were opened. The western compartment (to the left of the coffins) held a number of bamboo boxes, six of which held silk garments and fabrics. The boxes were tied with cords bearing clay seals inscribed "Majordomo of the Household of Marquis Dai" (above).

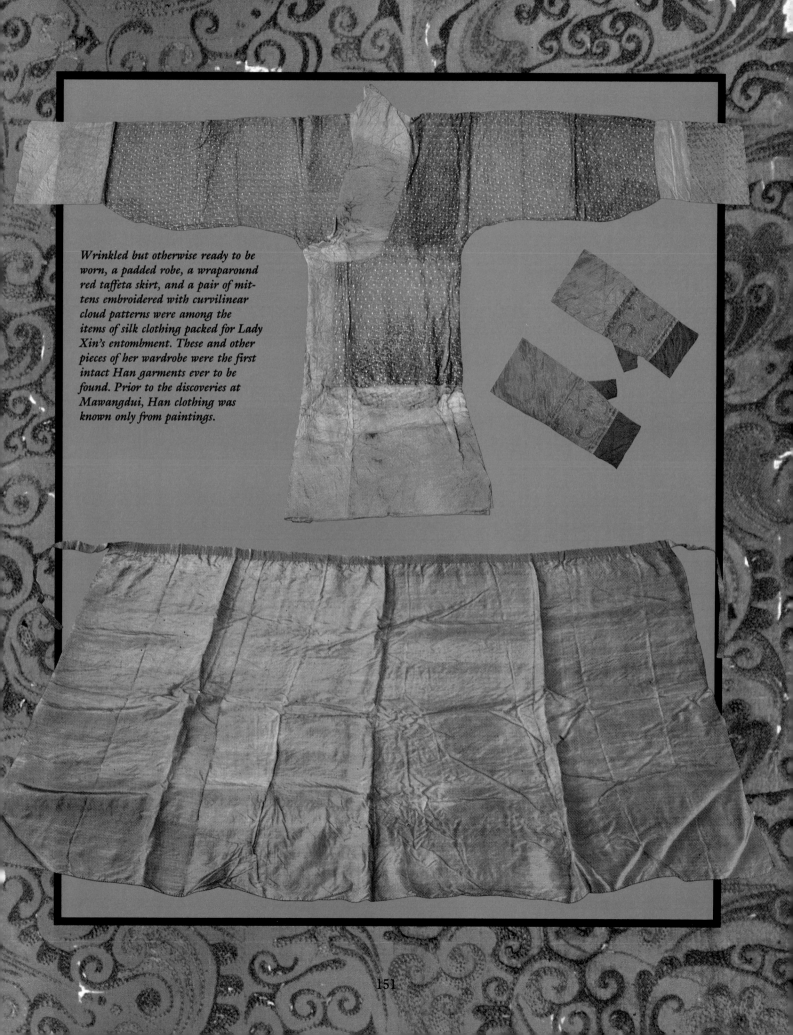

Wrinkled but otherwise ready to be worn, a padded robe, a wraparound red taffeta skirt, and a pair of mittens embroidered with curvilinear cloud patterns were among the items of silk clothing packed for Lady Xin's entombment. These and other pieces of her wardrobe were the first intact Han garments ever to be found. Prior to the discoveries at Mawangdui, Han clothing was known only from paintings.

FOOD FOR SUMPTUOUS FEASTS

The marquise of Dai enjoyed a high standard of cuisine from her chefs. Thirty bamboo cases and several dozen pottery containers held all the necessary ingredients for splendid feasts: rice, wheat, and lentils; lotus roots, strawberries, pears, dates, and plums; pork, venison, beef, lamb, hare, and dog; goose, duck, chicken, pheasant, turtledove, sparrow, crane, and owl; carp, bream, perch, and mandarin fish—presumably fresh caught from the family's own fish ponds. There were packets of spices and aromatics to flavor the food and jugs that probably held the wine to wash everything down. Nor was this all: Jotted on the 312 bamboo slips listing the contents of the tomb were extensive notes on fundamental culinary principles; favored ingredients; such seasonings as soy, honey, and salt; classic recipes; and cooking and preserving techniques not unlike those that are still in use today. Food could be roasted, sautéed, deep fried, steamed, or scalded, and meat and fish could be set aside for the future through salting, pickling, and sun drying. The bamboo slips even made mention of various desirable cuts, ranging from deer and dog flank to beef lips and tongue. Although one slip refers to the presence in a specific vessel of horsemeat, a favorite in Han China, none of it was found in Lady Xin's tomb.

The discovery of this wide assortment of comestibles and recipes has provided modern scholars with an incomparable insight into the food and drink of the Han's ruling elite—whose rich and varied diet was in stark contrast to the meager fare of common folk and their subsistence diet of wheat, millet, barley, or soybeans.

The conspicuous consumption of the upper classes was something of a scandal even in its day. Conservative Han commentators deplored such wanton practices as the taking of game out of season and the killing of baby fish and fledgling fowl in order to put novel delicacies on aristocratic tables. And the lavish banquets of the rich were unfavorably compared to the moderate meals of earlier times when wine and meat were served only at festivals and even the nobility used restraint in the slaughtering of animals.

A lacquerware tray laid with an ample meal sits in the silk-draped northern compartment of the burial chamber. Lacquered serving dishes—also seen opposite, empty—contain chicken drumsticks, spareribs, and morsels of fish—desiccated but still recognizable some 21 centuries after they were prepared. Slender chopsticks, neatly lined up, lie ready to be lifted by a ghostly hand.

Forty eggs survived the centuries in a 19-inch-long bamboo case (right). Other containers held fruits such as plums and the withered pears at lower right. Of 48 bamboo cases in the tomb, 30 held foodstuffs; the others were packed with textiles, herbal medicines, and household furnishings.

The set of dishes for the marquise's funerary meal represents the finest kind of tableware found in wealthy homes of the day. They are made of lacquered wood, black on the outside, red on the interior, and painted with decorative motifs. An oval cup with a pair of crescent-shaped handles is inscribed inside with characters that say, "May you enjoy this drink of wine." A 25-inch-long ladle was designed to reach the last drops deep inside a wine-storage jug.

A FORTUNE IN LACQUERWARE

Like the sumptuous silks and the rich foods, the 182 lacquered items found in the marquise of Dai's tomb testify to the taste for expensive luxuries among the status-conscious elite of the Western Han. Lacquered objects were regarded as the most precious of all manufactured goods—their value greater by far than that of equivalent items made of bronze. According to one contemporary text, it could take as many as 100 artisans to craft the thin wood base and apply the multiple layers of gleaming lacquer and intricate decoration to produce a single fine Han lacquered cup.

The lacquered housewares entombed with the marquise constitute the largest and most diverse collection of this precious commodity ever found. In addition to the plates, bowls, and trays off which the marquise dined, it includes vases, basins, armrests, toilet boxes, and small screens used decoratively and as protection against drafts.

Thanks to the tomb's uniquely humid atmosphere, the collection is also among the most perfectly preserved lacquer ever unearthed. While most old lacquerware eventually succumbs to dryness—shriveling and crumbling into dusty fragments—the marquise's ware, sitting out the centuries in air that one archaeologist characterized as "supersaturated," was virtually waterlogged, and it remained as lustrous as the day it was sealed inside the crypt.

This 20¼-inch-high squared container for wine was among the lacquered vessels packed in one of the tomb's side compartments (below). *Many of the items are inscribed: "Household of the Marquis of Dai."*

Some of the cosmetics and accessories used by high-ranking Han ladies were packed in a partitioned cosmetic case 14 inches in diameter. The upper compartment held a scarf, a belt, a mirror case, and three pairs of silk mittens. The nine small boxes in the lower compartment contained powder, rouge, hair ornaments, combs, brushes, and a long hairpiece.

Wooden toilet articles essential to maintaining a well-groomed appearance included, from left to right, a bristle makeup brush, a decorated hairpin, a pair of tweezers, and a fine-toothed comb.

A lacquered tripod called a ding was used to store food or as a service piece—perhaps to dish up bowls of geng, a kind of stew that was the basic meal in Han times. The shape of the vessel is taken from the traditional design of bronze vessels used to heat food over a hot fire.

PROVIDERS OF PLEASURES UNTOLD

Along with her extravagant furnishings, the marquise was buried with 162 carved wooden figures representing the large retinue of servants who had made her life so pleasant. Most of the effigies were small, painted statuettes, 18 to 20 inches high, probably representing workers who performed such duties as keeping house, tending crops and animals, working in the kitchens, and performing countless other tasks.

Eighteen larger figurines, some standing over 30 inches tall and clad in fabric outfits, evidently represented servants of higher rank. Two well-dressed menservants may have been household officials. Ten silk-clad females were apparently close personal attendants or ladies-in-waiting. And eight other large statuettes were musicians and dancers, reflecting Lady Xin's fondness for music and the premium Han aristocrats put on musical entertainment.

The wealthy of Changsha obviously hoped that, by carrying such retinues with them, they would find solace in the afterlife. Yet in the rich literary tradition of their region were disquieting images suggesting otherwise. The underworld evoked in the ancient *Songs of Chu* was not a realm peopled with competent servants, efficient bureaucrats, and amusing entertainers but a dark place ruled by a bloody deity "with dreadful horns on his forehead,"

who lay in wait to pursue and rend mortal souls.

The old verses also had a lament for the dead that, while calling for the soul's return to the body, evoked the happiness of the mortal world: "O soul, come back, to leisure and quietness! Enjoy yourself in the land of Chu, tranquil and untroubled. Indulge your fancies, fulfil your wishes, let your mind be at ease. O soul, come back to pleasure that cannot be told." This was the gracious life Lady Xin knew—a land of pleasures to which she could never return. The sumptuous tomb and all its luxuries were but a pale and paltry reflection.

The silk-clad, 31-inch-tall statuette of a high-ranking manservant (right) *was laid in the tomb among smaller figures in painted garb* (below). *In a departure from the more ancient practice of sacrificing servants upon the death of their masters or mistresses, such figures were substitutes for live retainers.*

A *chamber ensemble of foot-high, carved wooden musicians* (below) *play tiny replicas of the instruments with which their living counterparts entertained the Dai household. Three of them play zithers; two blow on mouth organs. The actual instruments, like the zither above and the mouth organ at right, were also included in the grave goods. The zither is strung with 25 strings wound on pegs and stretched over movable bridges. The mouth organ is composed of 22 bamboo pipes fitted into a wooden mouthpiece.*

AN UNBROKEN CHAIN OF TRADITION AND INVENTION

The vast expanse of China—from the western deserts and northern woodlands and riverine plains to the forests of the south—has been hospitable to human beings and their forerunners for approximately two million years. Its fertile plains were home to the hominid Lantian Man, identified from fossils believed to be 1.5 million years old, and a later *Homo erectus,* Peking Man, whose remains date back 500,000 years. Other finds suggest that *Homo sapiens* may have been present in China as early as 200,000 years ago. During Paleolithic times hunters, armed with stone weapons, tracked saber-toothed tigers, elephants, and other beasts.

The Neolithic era, beginning about 5000 BC, saw the rise of agriculture, the domestication of animals, and the creation of pottery—prototype for later cast-bronze vessels—whose abundant remains establish the locales of many Neolithic societies. Eventually separate tribal states—among them Shang—would emerge under the control of dynastic rulers. After 2,000 years of vying with one another, they would be united into a single empire by the kingdom of Qin; this development brought stability and helped spawn great technological and social innovations.

SHANG
c. 1700—c. 1050 BC

JADE FIGURINE

WESTERN ZHOU
c. 1050—771 BC

BRONZE VESSEL

Late in the third millennium BC, some Neolithic tribes learned to produce bronze. Subsequent cultures refined the process, thus ushering in the Bronze Age. Tribal states began to take shape under kings, and one such Bronze Age kingdom—Shang—came to dominate some of the others. In the 1930s Chinese archaeologists began unearthing a late Shang capital near Anyang, in Henan Province, where royal tombs were found. By the time the Shang moved to this city, they were casting bronze vessels of exquisite beauty.

Some of these bronzes bear names inscribed in a script that established the basic forms of the Chinese written language. The script is also found on tortoise shells and ox bones, which Shang kings used for divining. Religious as well as political leaders, these hereditary monarchs conducted sacred rituals. During important ceremonies and royal burials, sacrifices of human beings took place. The Shang also worshiped a supreme god, Shang Di.

During the Shang period the Chinese refined the art of silk making and created a high-fired ceramic ware and elaborate jade objects, such as the kneeling man above, found in the tomb of Fu Hao, King Wu Ding's consort, who may have led military campaigns on his behalf.

In a state on the western frontier of the Shang territory, a tribe known as the Zhou was led by kings whose armies launched a series of incursions into Shang territory. The Zhou monarch Wen Wang died in one such foray, around 1050, and shortly afterward, the ruler's son Wu Wang captured and laid waste to Anyang, forcing the last Shang king, Di Xin, to commit suicide. For the next 279 years, Wu Wang's successors would be called the Western Zhou dynasty, because their capital, near Xi'an in Shaanxi Province, was their first major power base.

After the conquest, Wu Wang parceled out both Shang and Zhou lands to subordinates to administer, marking the beginnings of a feudal system that would constantly expand. Vassals were expected to till the land they were given, supply troops to fight the barbarians, pay tribute to the king, and attend his court on a regular basis. Ceremonial music, poetry, art, and pageantry added to the majesty of the royal court. Throughout the territories ruled by the Zhou, new walled cities arose.

Jade objects became more refined, and the casting of bronze ritual vessels, such as the one above, was continued. Many carried inscriptions heralding events of importance to the king and the royal family.

EASTERN ZHOU
771—221 BC

QIN
221-206 BC

HAN
206 BC-AD 220

LACQUERED DEER

TERRA-COTTA KNEELING ARCHER

BRONZE HORSE

In 771 BC hordes of barbarians defeated the Zhou forces and destroyed their capital. The new ruler, Ping Wang, retreated eastward to Luoyang in Henan Province, there to establish a new capital. The era under this dynasty has thus become known as the Eastern Zhou. Vassal states, established by earlier Zhou kings, grew increasingly independent, until the Zhou monarchs functioned as ceremonial rulers only.

The Eastern Zhou epoch has traditionally been divided into two consecutive periods: The first, the Spring and Autumn era, ended in 481 BC and was followed by the Warring States period. Both of these were marked by a struggle for hegemony between the great states and the feudal lords. Warfare intensified, yet even as the states fought for supremacy, population was growing in the cities, where philosophy, literature, and crafts flourished and technology reached new heights. Ornaments such as the lacquered wood deer above proliferated, and finely detailed metalwork was possible with the introduction of the lost-wax method of production.

At the beginning of the Eastern Zhou period, some 170 states had existed. As the era drew to a close, most had been swallowed up by seven large states, poised for a final showdown.

Of the seven surviving states in the third century BC, it was the western state of Qin that triumphed over the others, under the able leadership of King Zheng and his adviser Li Si. In 221 BC Zheng declared himself Qin Shihuangdi, or First August Emperor, and the unification he imposed on the states he conquered indeed marked a new epoch in Chinese history. He now ruled a state extending from the East China Sea to the foothills of the Himalayas, north to the border of today's Inner Mongolia, and south to the boundary of present-day Vietnam. His capital was Xianyang near the current Xi'an.

The First Emperor rejected a return to feudal customs, imposing a tight centralized control over the empire. To regulate trade, he standardized coins as well as weights and measures and decreed a single form of written language. His many public works included a system of roads and a northern defensive wall. He built himself an enormous palace and a treasure-laden tomb. Life-size terra-cotta figures of his army, such as the one above, found in pits near his tomb, reveal much about the strength and strategies of his potent fighting force. His death in 210 BC led to civil wars ending in 206 with the establishment of the Han dynasty.

A commander of rebel forces, Liu Bang founded the Han dynasty. The central bureaucracy was strengthened and recruitment into its ranks was based on merit.

During the second century BC, Emperor Wu opened an overland trade route to the West, controlled by government officials, which would gain fame as the Silk Road. Chinese silk was in demand throughout Asia and in the Middle East and Europe; in exchange came gold, horses, camels, perfumes, and other desirable items.

Cast iron and steel, mass produced in government foundries, replaced bronze weapons and tools, although many ornaments continued to be made of bronze, such as the graceful galloping horse above. Brilliantly colored lacquer work and ceramics reached a high level of excellence. Around AD 105 paper was invented.

Han rule was interrupted in AD 9 after factional fighting brought to power Wang Mang, nephew of the dowager empress. But Wang Mang was overthrown in AD 23, and Han rule was restored. The capital moved east from Chang'an to Luoyang in Henan Province, and the period has become known as the Eastern, or Later, Han. By the time the dynasty fell in AD 220, China had become powerful and prosperous and a major force in Asia.

ACKNOWLEDGMENTS

The editors are especially grateful to Madame Wang Limei, deputy director of the Foreign Affairs Division of the Cultural Relics Bureau, and the bureau's staff in the People's Republic of China for their invaluable assistance in the preparation of this volume. The editors also wish to thank the following individuals and institutions: Massimo Baistrocchi, Rome; Chang Liantai, China Pictorial, Beijing; W. T. Chase, Freer Gallery of Art, Washington, D.C.; R. A. Crighton, Fitzwilliam Museum, Cambridge; Ursula Didoni, Linden-Museum, Stuttgart; Danielle Elisseeff, Rédactrice de la Revue Bibliographique de Sinologie,

E.H.E.S.S., Paris; Laveta A. Emory, Arthur M. Sackler Gallery, Washington, D.C.; Anne Farrer, British Museum, London; Feng Haojiang, The Institute of Archaeology, Chinese Academy of Social Sciences, Beijing; Keita Fujimoto, Asahi Shimbun, Tokyo; Valérie Gagliano, Les Dossiers d'Archéologie, Dijon; April Goebel, National Geographic Society, Washington, D.C.; Guo Weifu, Cultural Relics Publishing House, Beijing; Günter Heil, Berlin; Colleen Hennessey, Arthur M. Sackler Gallery, Washington, D.C.; Patricia Kattenhorn, British Library, London; Thomas Lawton, Freer Gallery of Art, Wash-

ington, D.C.; Liu Suchen, China Pictorial, Beijing; O. Louis Mazzatenta, National Geographic, Washington, D.C.; Jessica Rawson, British Museum, London; Ren Lingjuan, New World Press, Beijing; Karen Richter, Princeton University, Princeton, New Jersey; Sun Yarong, Cultural Relics Publishing House, Beijing; Peter Thiele, Linden-Museum, Stuttgart; Tian Hong, Time Magazine, Beijing; Nadia Tumiati, Foto-Grafica s.r.l., Rome; Yang Jin, Cultural Relics Publishing House, Beijing; Yao Furong, China Pictorial, Beijing; Zhao Haisheng, State Bureau of Cultural Property, Foreign Affairs Office, Beijing.

PICTURE CREDITS

Cultural Relics Publishing House, Beijing. 63: From the Arthur M. Sackler Collections, photograph courtesy of the Arthur M. Sackler Foundation. 64: Calligraphy by Dr. Shen Fu, Senior Curator of Chinese Art, Freer Gallery of Art and Arthur M. Sackler Gallery, Smithsonian Institution, Washington, D.C.—The Institute of Archaeology, Chinese Academy of Social Sciences, Beijing. 65: Cultural Relics Publishing House, Beijing. 67: Prof. Dr. Peter Thiele, Director, Linden-Museum, Stuttgart, Germany. 70: Cultural Relics Publishing House, Beijing. 72: Copyright British Museum, London. 73: Asahi Shimbun, Tokyo. 74, 75: The State Bureau of Cultural Relics, Beijing (2); Asahi Shimbun, Tokyo; The State Bureau of Cultural Relics, Beijing. 76, 77: The State Bureau of Cultural Relics, Beijing. 78: Asahi Shimbun, Tokyo—The State Bureau of Cultural Relics, Beijing. 79: The State Bureau of Cultural Relics, Beijing. 80, 81: The State Bureau of Cultural Relics, Beijing; copyright British Museum, London; The State Bureau of Cultural Relics, Beijing (3). 82: Daniel Schwartz, Zurich. 84: From *Jenseits der Grossen Mauer,* Bertelsmann Lexikon Verlag, Munich, 1990/courtesy Shaanxi Archaeological Overseas Exhibition Corporation, Xi'an. 86, 87: Daniel Schwartz, Zurich. 88, 89: From *Jenseits der Grossen Mauer,* Bertelsmann Lexikon Verlag, Munich, 1990/courtesy Shaanxi Archaeological Overseas Exhibition Cor-

poration, Xi'an. 91: From *Jenseits der Grossen Mauer,* Bertelsmann Lexikon Verlag, Munich, 1990/courtesy Shaanxi Archaeological Overseas Exhibition Corporation, Xi'an—Daniel Schwartz, Zurich. 92, 93: The National Museum of Chinese History, Beijing. 94: China Pictorial, Beijing. 95: Art by Time-Life Books. 96: Seth Joel, New York. 97: Shaanxi Archaeological Overseas Exhibition Corporation, Xi'an. 98, 99: From *The First Emperor of China,* by Arthur Cotterell, Macmillan London Ltd., 1981/ courtesy Shaanxi Archaeological Overseas Exhibition Corporation, Xi'an—Daniel Schwartz, Zurich. 100: Foto Claus Hansmann, Munich. 101: Bibliothèque Nationale, Paris. 102, 103: New World Press, Beijing. 105: Howard Nelson, London. 106, 107: China Pictorial, Beijing. 108, 109: Don Hamilton, Hamilton Photography & Film Co., Spokane, Wash. 110: New World Press, Beijing (2); Gianni Dagli Orti, Paris. 111: New World Press, Beijing. 112, 113: Seth Joel, New York; Seth Joel/Woodfin Camp & Associates; Seth Joel, New York; Gianni Dagli Orti, Paris (hand colored by Fred Holz). 114: The Nelson-Atkins Museum of Art, Kansas City, Mo. (Nelson Fund) 33-521. 117: The Institute of Archaeology, Chinese Academy of Social Sciences, Beijing (3)—China Pictorial, Beijing. 118-119: Map by Time-Life Books. 120-122: The Museum of the Western Han Tomb of the Nanyue King,

Guangzhou. 126: Cultural Relics Publishing House, Beijing. 128: China Pictorial, Beijing. 129: Courtesy of the Chinese Culture Center of San Francisco. 130: Cultural Relics Publishing House, Beijing. 132, 133: Asian Art and Archaeology. 134: Don Hamilton, Hamilton Photography & Film Co., Spokane, Wash. 137: The Institute of Archaeology, Chinese Academy of Social Sciences, Beijing. 138, 139: O. Louis Mazzatenta, © National Geographic Society. 143-145: China Pictorial, Beijing. 146, 147: Background China Pictorial, Beijing. Asian Art and Archaeology; China Pictorial, Beijing; art by Fred Holz; Asian Art and Archaeology. 148, 149: China Pictorial, Beijing; seeds, Hunan Provincial Museum, Changsha. 150, 151: Background China Pictorial, Beijing. Cultural Relics Publishing House, Beijing; China Pictorial, Beijing (4). 152, 153: Background China Pictorial, Beijing. Cultural Relics Publishing House, Beijing; China Pictorial, Beijing (4). 154, 155: Background China Pictorial, Beijing. Asian Art and Archaeology; Cultural Relics Publishing House, Beijing; Asian Art and Archaeology—China Pictorial, Beijing. 156, 157: Background China Pictorial, Beijing. Cultural Relics Publishing House, Beijing; China Pictorial, Beijing; China Pictorial, Beijing; Cultural Relics Publishing House, Beijing—China Pictorial, Beijing. 158, 159: Art by Paul Breeden.

BIBLIOGRAPHY

BOOKS

Andersson, J. Gunnar. *Children of the Yellow Earth: Studies in Prehistoric China.* Translated by E. Classen. Cambridge, Mass.: MIT Press, 1973.

Avrin, Leila. *Scribes, Script and Books.* Chicago: American Library Association, 1991.

Bagley, Robert W. *Shang Ritual Bronzes in the Arthur M. Sackler Collections.* Washington, D.C.: Arthur M. Sackler Foundation, Arthur M. Sackler Museum, Harvard University, 1987.

Ba Shu Bronze Ware. Compiled by the Provincial Museum of Sichuan. Sichuan, China: Chengdu Publishing House and Macau Sinobrothers, n.d.

Blunden, Caroline, and Mark Elvin. *The Cultural Atlas of the World: China.* Alexandria, Va.: Stonehenge Press, 1991.

Bodde, Derk. *China's First Unifier.* Hong Kong: Hong Kong University Press, 1967.

Bodde, Derk (trans.). *Statesman, Patriot, and General in Ancient China: Three Shih Chi Biographies of the*

Ch'in Dynasty. New Haven: American Oriental Society, 1940.

Buchanan, Keith, Charles P. FitzGerald, and Colin A. Ronan. *China*. New York: Crown Publishers, 1981.

Capon, Edmund. *Qin Shihuang: Terracotta Warriors and Horses*. Melbourne: Art Gallery of New South Wales and International Cultural Corporation of Australia Limited, 1982.

Capon, Edmund, and William Mac-Quitty. *Princes of Jade*. New York: E. P. Dutton, 1973.

Chang, K. C.:
The Archaeology of Ancient China (4th ed.). New Haven: Yale University Press, 1983.
Art, Myth, and Ritual: The Path to Political Authority in Ancient China. Cambridge, Mass.: Harvard University Press, 1983.
Shang Civilization. New Haven: Yale University Press, 1980.

Chang, K. C. (ed.). *Food in Chinese Culture: Anthropological and Historical Perspectives*. New Haven: Yale University Press, 1977.

Ch'ên, Shou-yi. *Chinese Literature: A Historical Introduction*. New York: Ronald Press, 1961.

Chêng Tê-K'un. *Archaeology in China, Volume 3: Chou China*. Cambridge: W. Heffer & Sons, 1963.

Christie, Anthony. *Chinese Mythology* (Library of the World's Myths and Legends series). New York: Peter Bedrick Books, 1987.

A Chronological Table of Chinese and World Cultures. Taipei, Taiwan: National Palace Museum, 1986.

Claiborne, Robert, and the Editors of Time-Life Books. *The Birth of Writing* (Emergence of Man series). New York: Time-Life Books, 1974.

Clayre, Alasdair. *The Heart of the Dragon*. Boston: Houghton Mifflin, 1984.

Cohen, Joan Lebold, and Jerome Alan Cohen. *China Today and Her Ancient Treasures* (2d ed.). New York: Harry N. Abrams, 1980.

Cotterell, Arthur. *The First Emperor of China*. London: Macmillan, 1981.

Cotterell, Yong Yap, and Arthur Cotterell. *The Early Civilization of China*. New York: G. P. Putnam's Sons, 1975.

Creel, Herrlee G. *The Origins of Statecraft in China, Volume 1: The Western Chou Empire*. Chicago: University of Chicago Press, 1970.

Crump, J. I. (trans.). *Chan-Kuo Ts'e*. Oxford: Clarendon Press, 1970.

The Cultural Atlas of the World: China. London: Andromeda Oxford, 1991.

d'Argencé, René-Yvon Lefebvre. *Bronze Vessels of Ancient China in the Avery Brundage Collection*. San Francisco: Asian Art Museum, 1977.

Deydier, Christian. *Chinese Bronzes*. Translated by Janet Seligman. New York: Rizzoli, 1980.

Elisseeff, Danielle, and Vadime Elisseeff. *New Discoveries in China: Encountering History through Archeology*. Translated by Larry Lockwood. Secaucus, N.J.: Chartwell Books, 1983.

Fessler, Loren, and the Editors of Life. *China* (Life World Library). New York: Time, Stonehenge Book, 1963.

Fidler, Sharon J., and J. I. Crump. *Index to the Chan-Kuo Ts'e*. Ann Arbor: Center for Chinese Studies at the University of Michigan, 1974.

The First Men (The Emergence of Man series). New York: Time-Life Books, 1973.

Fleming, Stuart J. *Authenticity in Art: The Scientific Detection of Forgery*. New York: Crane, Russak, 1975.

Fong, Wen (ed.). *The Great Bronze Age of China*. New York: Metropolitan Museum of Art and Alfred A. Knopf, 1980.

Fontein, Jan, and Tung Wu. *Unearthing China's Past*. Boston: Museum of Fine Arts, 1973.

Gascoigne, Bamber. *The Dynasties and Treasures of China*. New York: Viking Press, 1973.

Gaur, Albertine. *A History of Writing*. London: British Library, 1984.

Gems of China's Cultural Relics. Compiled by Editorial Committee of "Gems of China's Cultural Relics." Beijing: Cultural Relics, 1992.

Gernet, Jacques. *A History of Chinese Civilization*. Translated by J. R. Foster. New York: Cambridge University Press, 1982.

Gettens, Rutherford John. *The Freer Chinese Bronzes*. (Vol. 2). Washington, D.C.: Freer Gallery of Art, Smithsonian Institution, 1969.

Goepper, Roger. *Das Alte China*. Munich: C. Bertelsmann, 1988.

Han Zhongmin and Hubert Delahaye. *A Journey through Ancient China*. London: Muller, Blond and White, 1985.

Hay, John. *Ancient China*. Edited by Magnus Magnusson. New York: Henry Z. Walck, 1973.

Hook, Brian (ed.). *The Cambridge Encyclopedia of China*. New York: Cambridge University Press, 1991.

Hopkirk, Peter. *Foreign Devils on the Silk Road*. London: John Murray, 1982.

Hsu, Cho-yun. *Ancient China in Transition*. Stanford: Stanford University Press, 1965.

Hsu, Cho-yun, and Katheryn M. Linduff:
Journey into China. Washington, D.C.: National Geographic Society, 1987.
Western Chou Civilization. New Haven: Yale University Press, 1988.

Huang, Ray. *China: A Macro History*. Armonk, N.Y.: M. E. Sharpe, East Gate Book, 1988.

Hulsewé, A. F. P. *Remnants of Ch'in Law*. Leiden, Netherlands: E. J. Brill, 1985.

Hunan Provincial Museum and Institute of Archaeology, Academia Sinica. *The Han Tomb No. 1 at Mawangtui, Changsha*. Hunan Province, China: Heibonsha, 1976.

Jia Lanpo and Huang Weiwen. *The Story of Peking Man: From Archaeology to Mystery*. Translated by Yin Zhiqi. New York: Oxford University Press, 1990.

Keightley, David N. *Sources of Shang History: The Oracle-Bone Inscriptions of Bronze Age China*. Berkeley: University of California Press, 1978.

Keightley, David N. (ed.). *The Origins of Chinese Civilization*. Berkeley: University of California Press, 1983.

Knauth, Percy, and the Editors of Time-Life Books. *The Metalsmiths* (The Emergence of Man series). New York: Time-Life Books, 1974.

Lacquer: An International History and Illustrated Survey. New York: Harry N. Abrams, 1984.

Latourette, Kenneth Scott. *A Short History of the Far East*. New York: Macmillan, 1946.

Lau, Aileen (ed.). *Spirit of Han*. Singapore: Southeast Asian Ceramic Society and Sun Tree, 1991.

Lawton, Thomas (ed.). *New Perspectives on Chu Culture during the Eastern Zhou Period*. Washington, D.C.: Smithsonian Institution, Arthur M. Sackler Gallery, 1991.

Ledderose, Lothar, and Adele Schlombs (eds.). *Jenseits der Grossen Mauer: Der Erste Kaiser von China und Seine Terrakotta-Armee*. Munich: Bertelsmann, 1990.

Levenson, Joseph R., and Franz Schurmann. *China: An Interpretive History*. Berkeley: University of California Press, 1969.

Li, Dun J. *The Ageless Chinese: A History*. New York: Charles Scribner's Sons, 1965.

Li Chi. *Anyang*. Seattle: University of Washington Press, 1977.

Li Xueqin. *Eastern Zhou and Qin Civilizations*. Translated by K. C. Chang. New Haven: Yale University Press, 1985.

Loewe, Michael:
  Everyday Life in Early Imperial China during the Han Period, 202 BC-AD 220. New York: Dorset Press, 1968.
  The Pride That Was China (Sidgwick & Jackson Great Civilizations series). New York: St. Martin's Press, 1990.

The Magnificent Maya (Lost Civilizations series). Alexandria, Va.: Time-Life Books, 1993.

Merson, John. *The Genius That Was China*. Woodstock, N.Y.: Overlook Press, 1990.

Peoples and Places of the Past. Washington, D.C.: National Geographic Society, 1983.

Pirazzoli-t'Serstevens, Michèle. *The Han Dynasty*. Translated by Janet Seligman. New York: Rizzoli, 1982.

Qian Hao, Chen Heyig, and Ru Suichu. *Out of China's Earth: Archeological Discoveries in the People's Republic of China*. Edited by Patricia Egan. New York: Harry N. Abrams, 1981.

The Quest for Eternity: Chinese Ceramic Sculptures from the People's Republic of China. San Francisco: Los Angeles County Museum of Art and Chronicle Books, 1987.

Rawson, Jessica. *Ancient China*. London: British Museum, 1980.

Rawson, Jessica (ed.). *The British Museum Book of Chinese Art*. London: British Museum, 1992.

Recent Archaeological Discoveries in the People's Republic of China. Paris: UNESCO, 1984.

Schafer, Edward H., and the Editors of Time-Life Books. *Ancient China* (Great Ages of Man series). New York: Time-Life Books, 1967.

7000 Years of Chinese Civilization. Milan: Silvana Editoriale, 1983.

Shoten, Kadokawa (ed.). *A Pictorial Encyclopedia of the Oriental Arts, Volume 1: China*. New York: Crown, 1969.

Sivin, Nathan (ed.). *The Contemporary Atlas of China*. Boston: Houghton Mifflin, 1988.

Smith, Bradley, and Wan-go Weng. *China: A History in Art*. New York: Doubleday, 1979 (rev. ed.).

A Soaring Spirit (TimeFrame series). Alexandria, Va.: Time-Life Books, 1987.

Stein, Aurel. *Innermost Asia*. London: Clarendon Press, 1928.

Stockwell, Foster, and Tang Bowen (eds.). *Recent Discoveries in Chinese Archaeology*. Translated by Zuo Boyang. Beijing: Foreign Languages Press, 1984.

Stories from China's Past: Han Dynasty Pictorial Tomb Reliefs and Archaeological Objects from Sichuan Province, People's Republic of China. San Francisco: Chinese Culture Foundation of San Francisco, 1987.

Swann, Nancy Lee. *Pan Chao: Foremost Woman Scholar of China*. New York: Century, 1932.

Temple, Robert. *The Genius of China: 3000 Years of Science, Discovery, and Invention*. New York: Simon and Schuster, 1986.

Thorp, Robert L. *Son of Heaven Imperial Arts of China*. Seattle: Son of Heaven Press, 1988.

Thorp, Robert L., and Virginia Bower. *Spirit and Ritual: The Morse Collection of Ancient Chinese Art*. New York: Metropolitan Museum of Art, 1982.

Twitchett, Denis, and Michael Loewe (eds.). *The Cambridge History of China, Volume 1: The Ch'in and Han Empires, 221 B.C.-A.D. 220*. Cambridge: Cambridge University Press, 1986.

The Unearthed Cultural Relics from Lei Gu Dun, Sui Zhou, Hu Bei Province. Beijing: Museum of Chinese Historical Relics, 1984.

Vitiello, Gregory (ed.). *Archaeology in China*. South Melbourne: Macmillan, 1977.

Vollmer, John E., E. J. Keall, and E. Nagai-Berthrong. *Silk Roads, China Ships*. Toronto: Royal Ontario Museum, 1983.

Waldron, Arthur. *The Great Wall of China: From History to Myth*. Cambridge: Cambridge University Press, 1990.

Wang Zhongshu. *Han Civilization*. Translated by K. C. Chang. New Haven: Yale University Press, 1982.

Watson, Burton (trans.). *Records of the Grand Historian of China*. Translated from the *Shih chi* of Ssu-ma Ch'ien (Vols. 1 and 2). New York: Columbia University Press, 1961.

Watson, William. *Archaeology in China*. London: Max Parrish, 1960.

Watt, James C. Y. *The Arts of Ancient China*. New York: Metropolitan Museum of Art, 1990.

Wonders from the Earth: The First Emperor's Underground Army. San Francisco: China Books and Periodicals, 1989 (rev. ed.).

The World Atlas of Archaeology. New York: Portland House, 1985.

PERIODICALS

Asian Art. (Washington, D.C.), 1990, Vol. 3, no. 2.

Bagley, Robert W. "A Shang City in Sichuan Province." *Orientations* (Hong Kong), November 1990.

Chang, K. C. "Archaeology and Chinese Historiography." *World Archaeology* (London), 1981, Vol. 13, no. 2.

"Chinese Outcry against Scientific Spoliation." *Literary Digest* (New York), Nov. 2, 1929.

Creel, Herrlee Glessner. "Dragon Bones." *Asia* (New York), March 1935.

Elisseeff, Danielle. "History of Zhongshan." *Histoire et Archeologie* (Paris), February 1985.

Hall, Alice J. "A Lady from China's Past." *National Geographic,* May 1974.

Hall, Dickson. "Relics from Xinjiang." *Orientations* (Hong Kong), July 1981.

Liang Chi-chao. "Archaeology in China." *Annual Report of the Board of Regents of the Smithsonian Institution,* 1927.

Mazzatenta, O. Louis. "A Chinese Emperor's Army for Eternity." *National Geographic,* August 1992.

Pirazzoli-t'Serstevens, Michèle. "Les Débuts de l'Âge du Bronze." *Archéologia* (Paris), June 1973.

Qi, Chen Ying. "The Mountain Worship." *Histoire et Archeologie* (Paris), February 1985.

Rudolph, R. C. "Preliminary Notes on Sung Archaeology." *Journal of Asian Studies,* February 1963.

Topping, Audrey. "China's Incredible Find." *National Geographic,* April 1978.

Ward, Fred. "Jade—Stone of Heaven." *National Geographic,* September 1987.

Zong, Zheng Shao. "Gold and Silver in Laid Bronzes." *Histoire et Archeologie* (Paris), February 1985.

OTHER SOURCES

Chang, K. C. (ed.). "Studies of Shang Archaeology." Selected papers from the International Conference on Shang Civilization. New Haven: Yale University Press, 1982.

"Chinese Calligraphy." Leaflet. Washington, D.C.: Freer Gallery of Art, Smithsonian Institution.

"Chu Tomb No. 1 at Mashan in Jiangling." Abstract. Cultural Relics Publishing House, Beijing, n.d.

"Dian: A Lost Kingdom in China." Catalog. Zurich: Museum Rietberg, 1986.

The Freer Chinese Bronzes (Vol. 1). Catalog. Washington, D.C.: Freer Gallery of Art, Oriental Studies, No. 7, 1967.

Lawton, Thomas. *Chinese Art of the Warring States Period: Change and Continuity, 480-222 B.C.* Catalog. Washington, D.C.: Freer Gallery of Art, Smithsonian Institution, 1982.

"The Loulan Kingdom and the Eternal Beauty." Catalog. Research Center for the Culture and Archaeology of Sinkiang, 1992.

INDEX

rial era, 16; "Golden Age," 9-10; impact of political turmoil on archaeological work, 14, 27, 30; increased archaeological activity initiated by the People's Republic, 30-31; mandate of heaven, 34; nomadic and barbarian threats against, 12, 55, 69, 71, 87, 93; prehistoric settlements in, 158; technological innovations produced in, 129-131; unification of authority, 68, 71, 86-89, 159; variety of spoken dialects in, 63. *See also* Han dynasty, Qin dynasty, Shang dynasty, Tang dynasty, Zhou dynasty

Ching River: 60

Chu (feudal state): 44, 50, 51, 55, 62, 66, 69, 86, 88, 89, 92, 103

Columbia University: 14

Confucius: 9, 63, *67*, 120; career of, 66-67; standard edition of texts produced by Han scholars, 142

Creel, Herrlee Glessner: 22-24

Cui Shi: 128-129

Cuo (king): burial goods of, *59;* excavation of tomb of, *56, 57*

Currency: feudal state coinage, *92-93;* Han dynasty coinage, 125; Qin dynasty coinage, 90, 92, *93;* shells used as, 8, *52,* 92

D

Dai, marquise of: *See* Xin, Lady

Dai, marquis of: *See* Li Cang

Dan: excavations at, 55

Daodejing (The Way and Its Power): 67, 126

Deng (empress): 142

Di: 56, 57; warriors of, *52*

Discourses of the Warring States: 46

Di Xin: 158

Dong Zhuo: 144

Dong Zuobin: 30; and oracle bones, 21-22

Dou Wan: excavation of tomb of, 116, *117*

Dragon Boat Festival: 69

Duan Fang: *31*

Dunhuang: scrolls excavated at, 13

Durkee, Norman: 44

E

Early Han period: *See* Western Han period

Eastern Han period: 118, 130, 142, 159; stamped brick excavated from tomb, *129;* tombs, 15

Eastern Zhou period: 10, 34, 64; division into Spring and Autumn and Warring States periods, 46, 159; end of, 71; historical records of, 46-49; lacquerware, 66, 135, *159;* population growth, 60; production of gold, silver, and jade artifacts, 62-66; technological, artistic, and intellectual changes during, 46, 58-59, 62, 66-68; territorial boundaries, *map* 51; urbanization, 60-61; written script, 64. *See also* Spring and Autumn period and Warring States period

Erh Shihuangdi: 103, 104

Erlitou culture: 33

Eternal Beauty of Loulan: *76-77*

F

First Emperor: *See* Qin Shihuangdi

Freer Gallery of Art: 14, 15, 17, 22

Fu Hao: 20; excavation of tomb of, 8-9, 31, 158

Fu Sheng: 46

Fusu (prince): 101, 103

G

Gansu Province: 12, 18

Gobi Desert: 12

Gongxian: 130

Grand Canal: 60

Guangzhou: 120, 136

H

Han (feudal state): 60, 68, 88

Han dynasty: 10, 11; achievements of, 116-118; artisanship, regard for, 132-133; ban on human sacrifice, 120, 156; burial goods, *114,* 118-119, *121-122, 126, 128-130, 132-133, 134, 138-139, 141, 145-157;* capital cities, 16, 123, 124; clothing, *145;* court eunuchs, 143; daily life during, 119-123, 124-126, 127, 134; defensive walls built by, 136; development of central government bureaucracy, 123-124, 159; diet, 127, *152-153,* 155; diplomacy of, 137, 140; end of, 142-144; establishment of, 104, 123, 151; extent of empire, 118, 136-137; forced labor, 134-135, 137; gentry's growing wealth and social power, 115; government programs of social engineering, 124; historians, 49, 118; jade work, 120; kings, 115-116, 124, 135; lacquerware, 134-135, 146, *152-155,* 159; mass production of iron tools, 129-130; mer-

chant class, 118, 131-132; peasant cemetery, 119; riverboat, ceramic model of, *130;* saddlecloth, *81;* social structure, 132; and standard edition of Confucian texts, 142; tombs, excavation of and artifacts from, *145-157;* trade, 72, 80, 118, 136, 137-140, 159; wall tapestry, *80;* women, traditional role of, 140-142; wooden letter tablet, *81;* Yellow River flood-control projects, 135-136

Han Gou Canal: 60

Hangzhou: 60

Han River: 69

He (emperor): 141, 142

Hebei Province: 55, 56, 59, 68

Hedin, Sven: 12-13, 78; discovery of Loulan, 72

Helingeer (Inner Mongolia): excavations at, 127-128

Hemp: 127, 128

Henan Province: 14, 15, 16, 19, 33, 34, 43, 49, 68, 69, 119, 130, 134, 144, 158, 159

History of the Former Han: 118, 135, 142

Houma: 62

Huai River: 60

Huan (duke): 50

Huangdi (Yellow Emperor): 88, 89

Huan River: 7, 21

Hubei Province: 44, 47, 69, 91, 126

Huhai (prince): 101, 103. *See also* Erh Shihuangdi

Huixian: 55

Huizong (Song emperor): 12

Hunan Medical College: 149

Hunan Province: 66, 69, 126, 145

Hundred Schools of Thought: 66

Huns: 136

I

Imperial Hanlin Academy: 18

India: trade with, 140

Inner Mongolia: 127, 128

Inscriptions: 9, 19, 134; epitaphs, *137;* oracle bones, 20, 21, 26, 34, 64; and ritual bronze vessels, 12, 19, 34, 35, 37, 64

Institute of Archaeology (Beijing): 115

J

Jade: *6, 8, 12-13,* 28, 31, 39, 62-66, *158;* burial suit, 116, *117, 120-122;* Chinese regard for, 120; funerary mask, *32;* ornaments, *6, 12, 121;* ritual role in Neolithic burials, *12-*

R

Records of the Historian: 11, 49, 54, 60, 84, 88, 89, 93, 98, 100, 101, 103, 118

Religion: afterlife, 74, 75, 156; ancestor worship, 10, 11, 26, 35, 36; Buddhism, 13; Daoism, 126; divination, 19, 20, 98, 99, 158; human sacrifice, 8, 22, 24 25-26, 44, 47, 120; shamanism, 35, 41; Shang supreme diety, 26, 158; talismans, *75;* traditional beliefs, 100-101

Ren: 132

Rice: 127

River-Polished Stone: 56

Rome: and silk trade, 140

Rong: 93

Ruins of Yin: 7, 20

S

Sacred Circle and Kongque River burial barrow: *74-75*

Salt: government control over production of, 129

Sanmenxia: 34; funerary mask excavated at, *32;* iron sword excavated at, *32-33*

Sanxingdui: excavations at, *29;* Shang period artifacts excavated at, *28-29*

Seattle, Washington: exhibition of Chinese artifacts held at, 43-44

Seven Sorrows, The: 144

Shaanxi Institute of Archaeology: 139

Shaanxi Province: 12, 14, 16, 34, 60, 69, 83, 123, 131, 158

Shandong Province: 18, 50, 61, 65, 133, 144

Shang Di (deity): 26, 158

Shang dynasty: alcohol, 38; capital cities, 7, 21, 33; daily life during, 31; end of, 33-34; evidence of human sacrifice, 8, 22, 24-25, 26; executioner's ax, *25;* founding of, 33; jade work, 120; kings, 7, 11, 21, 99; lacquerware, 66, 135; metalworking, 26-27, 31, 35, 58; oracle bones used in royal divination, 19, 20; paucity of historical records, 9-10, 11-12; possible predecessor cultures, 33; ritual wine vessels, *38-41;* and Sanxingdui, 28; tombs, 8-9, *22-23,* 24-26, 158; writing, 31, 64, 158

Shanghai: 16

Shang Yang: 68, 86

Shanxi Province: 62, 68

Shi: philosopher-scholars, 67; role in government and military, 51, 53-54

Shiji: 84. *See also Records of the Historian*

Shu (feudal state): 60, 84

Sichuan Province: 28, 60, 129, 130, 140

Silk: advances in techniques of spinning and weaving, 66, 150, 158; clothing excavated from Chu kingdom tomb, *62,* 66; clothing excavated from Han tomb, *145,* 150, *151;* cultivation of, 128, 129; and manuscripts, *63,* 66, 131; trade in, 119, 140, 159

Silk Road: 72, 78, *map* 118-119, 159; early Western excavations along, 12-13

Sima Qian: 11, 21, 49, 116, 118, 132, 140

Sino-Japanese War: 18, 27

Smithsonian Institution: 22

Sogdiana, battle of: 94

Song (feudal state): 60

Song dynasty: Shang and Zhou dynasty relics compiled by, 11-12

Songs of Chu: 156

Soybeans: 34

Spring and Autumn Annals: 46

Spring and Autumn period: 46, 49; construction of defensive walls, 55; warfare during, 50, 51-53, 55-58, 69, 87, 159

Stein, Aurel: 18, 78; excavations at Dunhuang, 13; excavations at Niya, 81; mummified remains discovered by, *72*

Straight Road: 92-93

Stratagems of the Warring States: 71

Sumatra: Han trade with, 136

Sun Yirang: on oracle-bone inscriptions, 19

Sun Zi: 54

T

Tai ji chuan: 113

Taiwan University: 30

Taklamakan Desert: 12, 13, *map* 118-119; archaeological sites in, *72-81;* mummified remains found in, *72, 75, 76-77*

Tang dynasty: capital cities of, 16

Textiles: woolen clothing and spindle, *79. See also* Silk

Thorp, Robert L.: 116

Tiberius: 140

Tieshenggou: foundry of, 130

Tombs: Han dynasty, 15, 124, 125-126, 131, *145-157;* pilferage of, 10-11, 16, 18, 22, 24; Qin dynasty, 84-85, 93, *94-95, 102,* 104, *105-*

113; Shang, 8-9, *22-23,* 24-26; Warring States period, 52, 55, 56, 59; Zhou, 14

Tu Fang: 9, 20

Tutankhamen: 43

U

University of Pennsylvania Museum: 14

V

Vessels: riverboats, 130; rudder, use of, 130, 131

Vietnam: Han control in, 136

W

Wanchuan: 15

Wang Can: 144

Wangcheng: 49, 61

Wang Guowei: and oracle bones, 21

Wang Mang: 118, 159

Wang Yirong: 18-19

Warfare: arrowheads, *98-99;* cavalry, 52, 53, 71, 136, *143;* chariots, 51-53, 94, *102, 103;* conscription, 54, 68, 71; crossbows, 52, 58, 93-94, 98, 136; Eastern Zhou period, 46, 51-53, 87; Han period, 136; infantry, 53, 71; military units used as colonists, 127; Shang period, 31-33; soldiers of First Emperor, 93-95, *96, 97,* 98, *105, 110-113;* weaponry, improvements in, 55-58

Warring States period: 46, 52, 53-55, 126; consolidation of power during, 54, 159; estimate of casualties for, 54, 88; excavation of tombs dating from, 56, 59; final victory of Qin, 51, 69-71, 84; flood control and irrigation projects, 59-60; growth of cities, 61; iron, production and use of, 58-59; silk manuscript from, *63;* textile technology, advances in, 62; trade during, 61-62, 69

Way and Its Power, The (Daodejing): 67, 126

Wazhaxie: Neolithic site at, 14

Wei (feudal state): 52, 54, 55, 68, 85, 88, 89, 93

Wei River: 18, 89

Wen (emperor): 150

Wen Wang: 158

Western Han period: 118, 145, 154; written script, *65*

Western Zhou period: 10, 34, 46, 49, 158; administrative developments during, 34; bronze vessels, *30-31;* end of Zhou dynasty, 47; jade arti-

facts, *32;* lacquerware, 66; metal-working in, 35
Wheat: 127
Wheelbarrow: 130
White Di: 56
World War II: and disappearance of Peking Man, 18-19
Writing: brush, ink, and bamboo slips used for, *64,* 91; development and standardization of, 31, *63-65,* 90, 158, 159; paper and silk used for, 131
Wu (emperor): 140, 142, 143, 159; and expansion of Han power, 136-137
Wu, prince of: 59
Wu Ding: 9, 27, 158; oracle-bone inscription, 20
Wuguan: 25
Wu Wang (emperor): 158
Wuyuan: 128

X

Xi (Qin dynasty bureaucrat): excavation of tomb of, 91-92
Xiadu: excavations at, 59
Xia dynasty: 10, 33, 89
Xian (emperor): 144
Xi'an: 12, 16, 34, 46, 83, 123, 158
Xiang Yu: 104
Xianyang: 86, 103; imperial palaces at, *88, 89,* 90, 101, 104; sack of, 104
Xiao (duke): 68, 86
Xiaotun: 20, 21; tortoiseshell archive excavated at, 26-27
Xidajiaocun: excavation of convict graveyard at, 134-135, *137*

Xin, Lady (marquise of Dai): autopsy, *148-149;* excavation of tomb and artifacts from, 126, 127, *145-157;* funeral of, 146
Xinglong: excavations at, 59
Xiongnu: Han military campaigns against, 136, 137
Xuan (king): 67
Xun Qing: 87
Xunzi: 67

Y

Yan (feudal state): 53, 55, 59, 69, 88, 93, 100
Yang: 141
Yangshao culture: discovery of, 16-18; painted urns, *10-11*
Yangshaocun: Neolithic sites at, 16-18
Yangzi River: 34, 60, 69, 71
Yanshi: 33
Yanshi Xian: 134
Yellow Emperor: 88-89
Yellow River: 16, 53, 55, 143; Han flood-control projects on, 135-136
Yellow Turbans: 143-144
Yi (marquis): 50; burial goods, *42, 44, 45, 46, 47, 48;* tomb of, *47*
Yin: 141; Shang capital at, 7
Yu: 120. *See also* Jade
Yuezhi: 137
Yungang: 14
Yunjing: 15
Yunmeng: 91

Z

Zeng (feudal state): 44, 47, 50, 92
Zeng Hou Yi: *See* Yi (marquis)
Zhang: burial goods from tomb of,

143
Zhang brothers: peasant rebellion led by, 143-144
Zhang Qian: travels of, 137-140
Zhao (feudal state): 53, 54, 57, 68, 88, 93, 98, 116
Zhao Gao: 101, 103, 104
Zhao Guo: 129
Zhao Mo: excavation of tomb of, *121, 122;* jade burial goods of, *120-122*
Zheng (king): 87-88, 93, 159. *See also* Qin Shihuangdi
Zheng Guo: 60
Zheng Zhenxiang: 8
Zhengzhou: excavations at, 33
Zhongshan (feudal state): 56, 57, 60, 116
Zhou dynasty: abstemious nature of, 38; capital cities of, 16, 34, 46; destruction of Shang dynasty, 11, 30, 33-34; division into Eastern and Western Zhou periods, 46, 158; end of, 71; excavation of tomb sites from, 14; feudal government system, 49-50, 54, 158, 159; jade work, 120; kings, 49, 50, 69, 99; metalworking, 34, 35, 58-59; poetry, 36; social transformations during, 51, 86-87; swords, 58; traditional beginning of Chinese history, 10, 21; writing, 64. *See also* Eastern Zhou period, Western Zhou period
Zhoukoudian: fossil remains found at, 16, *18-19*
Zhuangxiang (king): 87
Zidanku: 66
Ziying (king): 104

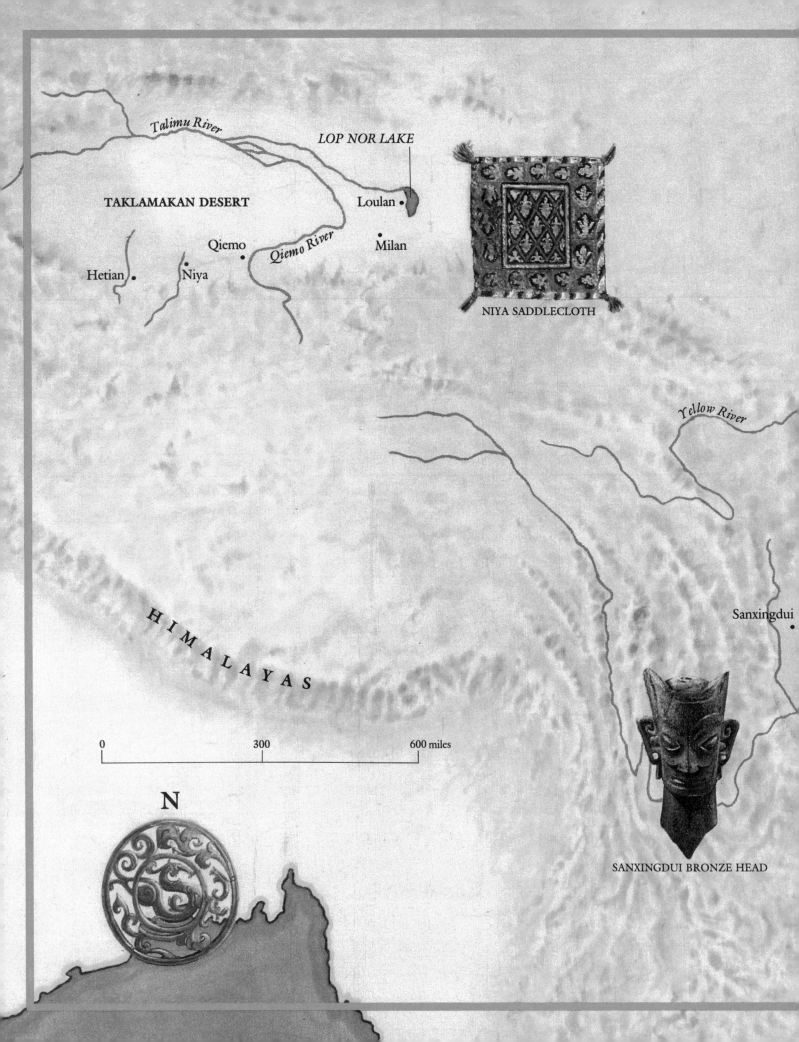

Talimu River

LOP NOR LAKE

TAKLAMAKAN DESERT

Loulan

Qiemo

Qiemo River

Milan

Hetian

Niya

NIYA SADDLECLOTH

Yellow River

Sanxingdui

HIMALAYAS

0   300   600 miles

N

SANXINGDUI BRONZE HEAD